I0009116

MAKING YOUR
WORDPRESS
SITE Awesome

The Intermediate Guide

First Edition

The Website Series - #2

Shere L.H. McClamb, Ph.D., PMP, PMI-ACP

First published: January 2018

Published by The bITa Group
Publishing@TheBitaGroup.com
Benson, North Carolina 27504

ISBN: 978-0-692-05251-8

Preface

Welcome to Making Your WordPress Site *Awesome - The Intermediate Guide* the second of *The Web Site Series* of books. The goal of the Intermediate Guide is to further equip those with limited web development experience with the skills and confidence to add the bells and whistles to their WordPress web site using an intermediate set of skills. Since 2003, WordPress has continued to provide thousands of web site creators with little web coding skills the ability to have awesome web site.

The cost of a WordPress site will increase if you decide to use premium WordPress themes or plugins. However, there are thousands of free WordPress themes and plugins available that you can use to reduce costs. You can add awesome features to your WordPress site using plugins without upgrading your hosting plan.

This is not a point and click manual, you've already experienced that in *Building a Web Site Using WordPress: The Beginner's Guide.* It is my hope that you will take the information provided in *Making Your WordPress Site Awesome - The Intermediate Guide,* you will develop a blueprint for your Web site's success.

Who is this book for?

- **Individuals** with limited or no coding experience who want to add the bells and whistles to their WordPress Web site.
- **Instructors** who are tasked with teaching intermediate WordPress.

Conventions

The following conventions are used to walk you through building a web site using WordPress:

- Step-by-step methodology.
- Using open-source resources.
- Tips around known pitfalls that may hinder progress.

Contents

What this book covers

CHAPTER ONE: Post and Page Management You will learn how to effectively represent the content on your site in a way that connects with your visitors.

CHAPTER TWO: User Management You will learn how to give both public facing and back-end users a full experience using and visiting your site.

CHAPTER THREE: Working with Dynamic Content You will learn intermediate-level skills that will allow you to create content in a more efficient way.

CHAPTER FOUR: A Site for Everyone You will learn to incorporate the elements to ensure your site is accessible based on respected web design standards groups.

CHAPTER FIVE: Being Social You will learn how to increase the visibility of your content using popular social channels and creating private forums.

CHAPTER SIX: Expanding your WordPress Footprint You will learn how improve engagement of your content by adding sub sites and other interactive elements to your site.

CHAPTER SEVEN: UX & UI You will learn how to display a look and feel that best represents and displays your content.

CHAPTER EIGHT: Menu Management You will learn how to structure an invaluable navigation tool for your content.

CHAPTER NINE: Site Optimization & Security You will learn how to enhance the experience of your visitors as they enjoy and interact with bandwidth-centric content and security of your site.

x

About the Author

Shere L.H. McClamb, Ph.D., PMP, PMI-ACP has more than 17 years working in the Information Technology field in the roles of Webmaster, Instructor, Instructional Technologies Developer, Business Systems Analyst, and Project Manager. She has taught at community and 4-year colleges as well as working for various governmental agencies within the State of North Carolina.

Shere holds a Ph.D. in Information Technology from Capella University, a Project Management Professional (PMP) and a Project Management Institute- Agile Certified Practitioner (PMI-ACP) Certifications from the Project Management Institute (PMI). She develops web sites and print media for her wonderful clients, teaches Web technologies and Project Management courses.

Thanks, I would like to thank my husband, Derrick, for his unwavering support for my many years of education and special projects. I would also like to thank my wonderful children (Todd, Danielle, Christopher, Daniel, and Ariannah) for cheering their Mom & Nana on as she stared at computer screens year after year.

CHAPTER ONE: POST AND PAGE MANAGEMENT

> *If your goal is to improve the look, layout, and access to the information in your site, learning the lessons of efficiency and affective placement is the best place to start. Content Matters.*

In this chapter, you will:

- Learn how use the WordPress text editor
- Learn how to use shortcuts and markdowns
- Learn how to use links in posts and pages
- Learn how to incorporate PDFs into posts and pages
- Learn about category management
- Learn about image management

WORKING WITH TEXT

Undeniably, most of your time will be spent creating content in the text editor. As an intermediate user, you will need to push further than knowing the basics of adding basic content to your pages and posts. Utilizing the text editor's many features will allow content to be created in a more efficient manner.

Utilizing the WordPress Text Editor

The WordPress visual editor is a WYSIWYG (**w**hat **y**ou **s**ee **i**s **w**hat **y**ou **g**et) editor. In this chapter, you will progress beyond the default layout built-in tools used in developing web site content. You are already familiar with the **formatting toolbar** located at the top of the WordPress text editor. By default, basic formatting elements of bold, italic, strikethrough, bulleting, numbering, horizontal line, align left, align center, align right, insert/edit link, remove link, insert read more tag, and the kitchen sink are displayed.

The Kitchen Sink Button

The **Kitchen Sink Button** toggles to show the additional line of formatting options of font sizes, underline, justify, font color, Paste (ctrl+v) as text, clear formatting, decrease indent, increase indent, undo, redo, and keyboard shortcuts.

The Kitchen Sink

SHORTCUTS

WordPress has added several shortcuts to formatting, headings, and lists. They are most commonly activated by using combinations of the:

- Control
- Alt
- Shift and
- Function keys

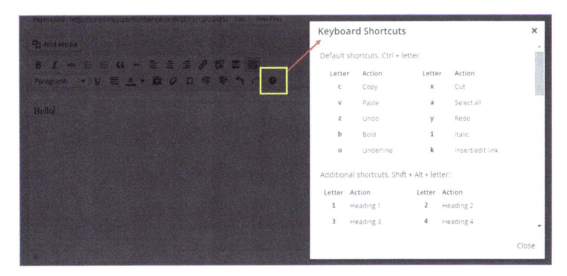

Text Patterns using Shortcuts

Type an asterisk (*) or a dash (-) to generate a bulleted list or Typing 1. or 1) to generate an ordered list.

Font Formatting Shortcuts

Typing the **greater-than symbol (>)** to generate a blockquote.
Starting a paragraph with **2 to 6 number symbols (#)** to generate different headings.

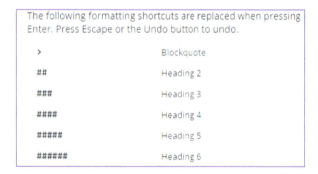

Focus Shortcuts

Focus shortcuts are initated by pressing the Alt button at the same time as a function button. Inline elements are further explained in the HTML books in the Creating Web sites Series.

Function8 *(F8)* to initiate focus on an inline element such as an image or a link.

Function9 *(F9)* focuses on the menu.

Function10 *(F10)* on the toolbar.

Function11 *(F11)* on the elements path.

Focus shortcuts:

Alt + F8   Inline toolbar (when an image, link or preview is selected)

Alt + F9   Editor menu (when enabled)

Alt + F10   Editor toolbar

Alt + F11   Elements path

To move focus to other buttons use Tab or the arrow keys. To return focus to the editor press Escape or use one of the buttons.

ADDING FUNCTIONALITY

WordPress is well known for giving users a stable platform to build a web site. It remains lightweight and user-friendly because it gives you what you need to get started in the installed version; it is up to you to create the backend that is unique to your needs allowing you to develop your site in a manner that is only limited by the backend tools you deploy as allies.

Spelling and Grammar

Well known for the lack of support for spelling and grammar functionality. In the latest updates there are queues to questionable spelling by use of red underlining. When the word is right-clicked the browser spell-check functionality gives options to correct possible mistakes.

These components have been shown in recent research to have a marked impayt on the OJP of IT professionals who work in organizations utilizing EA environments.

So what can you do other than writing content in a more robust text editor and then copying and pasting it into WordPress? The answer of course, is to go to the Codex at WordPress.org and search for a plugin that will help with spelling and grammar shortcomings.

When searching the term "spelling" in the WordPress plugin directory, over 300 variations of plugins that help with spelling in some way were found. When researching the spelling and grammar plugins that will work best for you notice that some even integrate spelling and grammar buttons into the formatting toolbar.

Columns

By default, WordPress does not have the functionality to create columns. Many premium themes come with column shortcodes in the formatting toolbar right out of the box.

If you do not have the ability to create columns in the toolbar with your theme, there is great news in the form of plugins. There are literally thousands of plugins that can be installed and used for free.

Tables

WordPress does not offer the ability to create tables, but of course there's a plugin for that too. I will leave it to you to search through all of free plugins available to create the type of table you need in the plugins directory on WordPress.org.

WORKING WITH LINKED INFORMATION AND MEDIA

Posts, pages, media, and external web site are connected by internal (somewhere on the same page) and external (on a different page or web site) links.

This is an example of a post with an internal link.

And here's a link with an external link ↗.

Links are basic functionality are created in several different ways. As you are well aware, basic links are created using the Insert/Edit link button on the formatting toolbar. Let's review the basics and move on to newer features, like 3rd Party Media Link (oEmbed) methods that will make linking your WordPress site to life outside the URL much easier.

Links: The Basics

You will use the same technique when creating a link within the same page, to another page within the site, or to another site.

STEP 1.   Highlight the text or image you want to make a link.

OJP is evaluated based (a) on successfully fulfilling the task (i.e., based on the criteria set by organizational expectations), and (b) contextual factors (i.e., the norms and rules shared by the members of the EA team on which an IT professional works) (Jensen et al., 2012). Success is ultimately determined based on an individual's ability to assimilate successfully within the confines of the behavioral patterns set by the organization (Dierdorff et al., 2012). Jensen et al. (2012) explained that resources can act as constraints that affect overall role

STEP 2.   Click on the **Insert/Edit Link** button.

criteria set by organizational expectations), and (b) contextual factors (i.e., the norms and rules shared by the members of the EA team on which an IT professional works) (Jensen et al., 2012). Success is ultimately determined based on an individual's ability to assimilate successfully within the confines of the behavioral patterns set by the organization (Dierdorff et al., 2012). Jensen et al. (2012) explained that resources can act as constraints that affect overall role performance of individuals as they aspire to successfully employ

STEP 3.   Fill in the information in the **Insert/Edit Link** text box.

URL: This is where you want the user to end up. This should be a full URL. This link can open anything in the media library with a URL. This is a very popular way to add PDF documents to the site.

Link Text: The text you highlighted in step 1.

Choosing the destination for your link.

1. Type the full (http://xxx.xxx) URL into the textbox.

2. Lookup previously created content by searching on keywords.

3. Choose the page or post you want to link to.

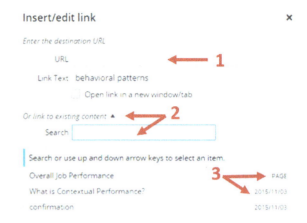

STEP 4. Choose whether the new page will:

- Replace the current page,
  Or
- Open in a new window or tab.

STEP 5. Click on the dropdown list to show the posts and pages currently saved in your site.

Insert/edit link   ✕

Enter the destination URL

       URL

  Link Text behavioral patterns

        ☐ Open link in a new window/tab

Or link to existing content ▲

    Search [   ]

Search or use up and down arrow keys to select an item.

Overall Job Performance	PAGE
What is Contextual Performance?	2015/11/03
confirmation	2015/11/03
Sample Page	PAGE
Hello world!	2015/10/19

Cancel   →   [Add Link]

STEP 6.   Type in a URL or choose one of the pages or posts and click the **Add Link** button to create the link.

norms and rules shared by th
professional works) (Jensen e
on an individual's ability to a
behavioral patterns set by th
(2012) explained that resourc
performance of individuals a

Result: A link of the text is created.

Copy and Paste (ctrl+v) Method

The copy and Paste (ctrl+v) method is as straightforward as it sounds. Simply copy (ctrl+c) the oEmbed supported URL from the browser bar and Paste (ctrl+v) in right into the post or page content area. Hit the enter key to create the link.

A clever reverse on this functionality are plugins like **CopyLink** that creates a link back to your web site when text is copied from your posts and pages.

3rd Party Media Link (oEmbed)

The oEmbed method works with most of the popular media sites. The whitelist containing the supported sites can be found in the Codex.

STEP 1.   Copy *(ctrl+c)* the URL of the media you want to embed into your site.

STEP 2.   Navigate to a clear line (free of any other content).

STEP 3.   Paste *(ctrl+v)* the URL of the media on the screen where you want the video to display.

🔒 https://www.youtube.com/watch?v=jaNVNUa67nE

STEP 4.   Press the **enter** key so that the URL is the only content on the line.

Result: WordPress will automatically turn the URL into a video embed with a preview provided.

If the media you want to emded into your post or page is not on the WordPress whitelist you can use the alaternative oEmbed shortcode wrapper around your media link.

STEP 1.   Copy *(ctrl+c)* the URL of the media you want to embed into your site.

STEP 2.   Navigate to a clear line (free of any other content).

STEP 3.   Paste (ctrl+v) the URL of the media on the screen where you want the video to display.

STEP 4.   Place your cursor at the beginning of the URL and type **[embed**

STEP 5.   Press the space key and type **width="#"**

STEP 6.   Press the space key and type **height="#"]**

STEP 7.   One the right side of the URL, close the embed shortcode by typing **[/embed]**

Result: A complete embedded wrapped media URL.

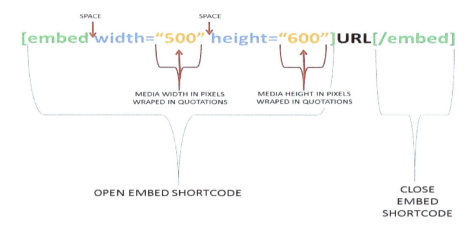

STEP 8.   Press the enter key so that the URL is the only content on the line.

Result: WordPress will turn the embedded wrapped URL into a video with a preview provided.

Removing a Link or an Embed

STEP 1.   Highlight the **link text** or **embedded media**.

professional works) (Jensen et al., 2012). Success is ultimately determined based on an individual's ability to assimilate successfully within the confines of the behavioral patterns set by the organization (Dierdorff et al., 2012). Jensen et al.

contextualperformance.com/.../what-is-contextual-performance ✏ ✕ ect overall role

performance of individuals as they aspire to successfully employ organizationally acceptable behavioral patterns.

STEP 2.   Click on the ⊠ at the end of the link.

on an individual's ability to assimilate successfully within the co behavioral patterns set by the organization (Dierdorff et al., 2012

contextualperformance.com/.../what-is-contextual-performance ✏ ✕ ect

performance of individuals as they aspire to successfully employ organizationally acceptable behavioral patterns.

Remove

Or click the x that appears on the embed itself

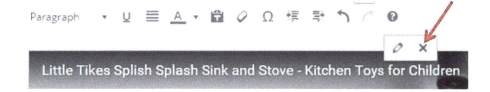

WORKING WITH PDFs

Working with PDF documents has become pretty commonplace. Taking advantage of this document type to display or as a download option is the current user-preferred method.

PDFs can be used in a WordPress site in a few different ways.
- **A text link** can open a pdf document to replace the current page
- **A link that opens in a new window**, and
- **Embedded** and become the content of the page

PDF's The Basics

Creating a link to a PDF document from your Media Library:

STEP 1.   Navigate to the **Media Library** and open the PDF document you want to create a link to.

STEP 2. Find the **File URL text box.**

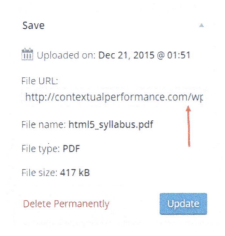

STEP 3.   Copy (ctrl+c) the entire link (it should end with.pdf).

STEP 4.   Paste (ctrl+v) in the File URL: box

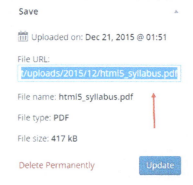

STEP 5. Close the Media Library.

STEP 6. Highlight the text or image you want to make a link.

STEP 7. Click on the Insert/Edit Link button.

STEP 8. In the Insert/Edit Link URL textbox, Paste (ctrl+v) the PDF's URL.

STEP 9. Fill in the information in the Insert/Edit Link text box (#2).

STEP 10. Choose whether the PDF will replace the current window or open in a new window or tab (#3).

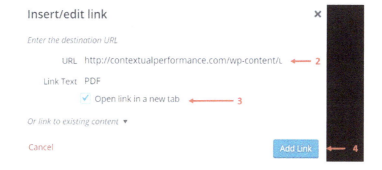

STEP 11. To complete creating the link, click the **Add Link** button (#4).

Embedding a PDF into a Post or a Page

With the use of embedding plugins, you can use the embed shortcode to embed a PDF into your post or page. Popular PDF embed plugins work similarly to embed media using short codes.

There are at this time more than 79 hits returns when searching on the terms embedding PDFs.

For example:
Install the PDF embedder of your choice, in this example, I used PDF embedder.

STEP 1.   Copy (ctrl+c) the **URL** of the PDF from the Media Library.

STEP 2. Navigate to a clear line (free of any content) in your post or page.

STEP 3. Paste (ctrl+v) the URL of the PDF on the screen where you it to display.

STEP 1. Go to the **Media Library**.

STEP 2. Choose the PDF you want to embed.

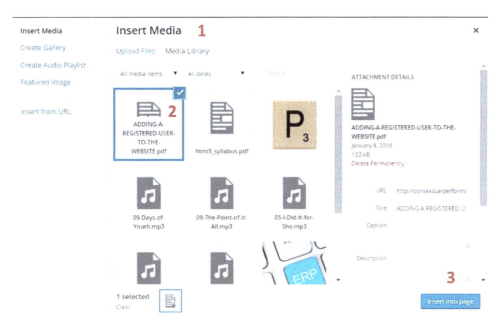

STEP 3. Click on the **Insert into page** button.

The width and height is not required in the shortcode when embedding a PDF. The PDF's dimensions are most likely to be configured in the plugin's settings.

Result: A completely embed-wrapped PDF document URL.

[pdf-embedder url="http://contextualperformance.com/wp-content/uploads/2016/01/ADDING-A-REGISTERED-USER-TO-THE-WEBSITE.pdf"]

STEP 4.   Click on a preview option or publish the post or page to view the PDF.

Result: WordPress will turn the wrapped URL into an embedded PDF.

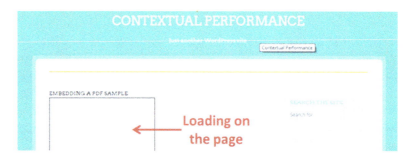

POSTS

Posts are a staple of your WordPress web site. Utilizing built-in WordPress elements such as good titles, post tags, and post formats will make creating content more accessible, interesting, and user-friendly.

Using Post Tags

Even though using post tags is an introduction-level element, it is important and garners a place in an intermediate post section. Post Tags are keywords for Posts. Users will use these words to find posts in the site. Once a tag is created, it can be used for multiple posts.

To add tags to a post:

STEP 1. Place your cursor in the Tags textbox.

Tags

[   ] Add

Separate tags with commas

Choose from the most used tags

STEP 2. Type the tag title.

Tags

[Servant Leadership] Add

Separate tags with commas

Choose from the most used tags

STEP 3. Click the **Add** button.

Tags

[   ] Add

Separate tags with commas

☼ Servant Leadership

Choose from the most used tags

Result: The new tag will appear

Removing Tags from a Post:

To remove a tag, click the **Delete** button next to the tag.

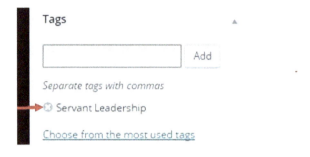

Custom Fields

I am going to be straight with you here. This is not an easy concept to understand or implement. These fields are used to add additional meta-data *(data about the data)* to your post. This metadata can be used to accomplish some really cool stuff. For instance, one could set a date for a WordPress Post to expire, display custom headers, footers, sidebars, or even manipulate the RSS feed content.

In order for this to work, custom fields must be placed in name (key)/value pairs. Keys are the drivers of the metadata pair and can be reused with different values, but the value is what shows in the meta-data listing. You will need to use the **excerpt template tag**. Plugins are available for easier administration of custom fields. Many post authors find it helpful to add additional information about the posts in the form of meta-data. The key (name)/value pair is used to enter information that can help to identify and group posts.

Adding Custom fields is a somewhat complicated 2-part process. The first is to add the custom field pair to the post screen. The second is to call it in the post.

PART I

This can get confusing fast, so let me define a few terms before explaining how to move forward.

1. **MetaData** - the data used to describe data (yea, I know!). Custom fields are a way to describe posts (data about data).

2. **Key** - identifies the specific field. This is the primary word (metadata) that will be used to describe the post (data). This key can be used on multiple posts. Particularly useful if your intent is to group a set of post is some way.

3. **Value** - descriptive information for the key field. Once you have you primary, name, or key, the value serves as a description of the data.

In order for the custom fields section to show on the Post screen:
    STEP 1.   Choose screen options.
    STEP 2.   Check the **custom fields** option.

PART II

Add the following code to the **single.php** file.

STEP 1. Hover over the **Appearance** link in the left main menu and then click the **Editor** link from the submenu.

Result: The edit page with the links to the site templates displays.

University: Single Post (single.php)

```php
<?php get_header(); ?>

<div id="contentwrapper">
  <div id="content">
    <?php while ( have_posts() ) : the_post(); ?>
    <div <?php post_class(); ?>>
      <h1 class="entry-title">
        <?php the_title(); ?>

      </h1>
      <div class="entry">
        <?php the_content(); ?>
        <?php wp_link_pages(); ?>
        <?php echo get_the_tag_list('<p class="singletags">',' ','</p>'); ?>
        <?php comments_template(); ?>

      </div>
    </div>
    <?php endwhile; // end of the loop. ?>
  </div>
  <?php get_sidebar(); ?>
</div>
<?php get_footer(); ?>
```

STEP 2.   Click on the **Single Post** link in the **Templates** menu.

STEP 3.   Paste *(ctrl+v)* the following code into the beginning of the. php code of the page.

```
1    <?php the_meta(); ?>
```

or place a more complicated version in the WordPress loop:

```
University: Single Post (single.php)

<?php get_header(); ?>

<div id="contentwrapper">
  <div id="content">
    <?php while ( have_posts() ) : the_post(); ?>
    <div <?php post_class(); ?>>
      <h1 class="entry-title">
        <?php the_title(); ?>

      </h1>
      <div class="entry">
        <?php the_content(); ?>
<?php wp_link_pages(); ?>
        <?php echo get_the_tag_list('<p class="singletags">',' ','</p>'); ?>
        <?php comments_template(); ?>

      </div>
    </div>
    <?php endwhile; // end of the loop. ?>
  </div>
  <?php get_sidebar(); ?>
</div>
```

```
1    <?php echo get_post_meta($post->ID, 'key', true); ?>
```

STEP 4.   Click on the **Update File** button to save your changes.

Fortunately, there are many great templates and plugins that help simplify creating and deploying custom fields!

If working with custom fields was difficult for you. There is both good and bad news - there were over 1,000 plugin results returned when searching on the terms custom fields.

Some of the most highly rated custom field plugins taut the fact that you will be more easily create, modify, and deploy. Pack your patience!

Making Posts, Headers, Menus, and Banners Sticky

Sticky is a cool word for the tactics you will use to encourage web site visitors to not only 'stick' around, but will also encourage them to return. Having a site that is timely, well developed and relevant are foundation stickiness, but this chapter will help you can take it further. Branding your web site with memorable logos and taglines have the ability to draw favor with visitors. For others it will be the ease in which you answer their questions with text or images. Visitors feel engaged if they can imagine where you are in the world or at the least, how they can contact you. Most web sites have contact information in the header or footer of their pages in addition to a link to a dedicated contact page.

It is a mistake to overlook making your WordPress site social. In addition to thousands of social plugins, most templates come with the most popular social sites integrated into their design. If for some reason you are not a participant in the social revolution you should at the least have the ability for site registration, email newsletters. In other words – engagement is essential. One way you can make you web site sticky is making your posts sticky.

Making a WordPress Post Sticky

STEP 1.   Open the post you want to make sticky.

STEP 2.   Click on the **Edit** link beside visibility in the Publish section of the posts screen.

STEP 3.   Place a checkmark in the **Stick this post to the front page**.

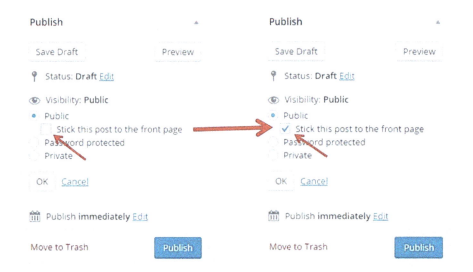

Useful Sticky Plugins

Making posts sticky

Sticky Post

A plugin for displaying sticky posts based on custom taxonomy, order, and much more.

By zourbuth

Install Now

More Details

 (2)

1,000+ Active Installs

Last Updated: 3 years ago

Untested with your version of WordPress

To set a sticky post to expire on a special date and time there is a popular sticky post.

Expire Sticky Posts

A simple plugin that allows you to set an expiration date on posts. Once a post is expired, it will no longer be sticky.

By Andy von Dohren

Install Now

More Details

(0)

300+ Active Installs

Last Updated: 1 year ago

Untested with your version of WordPress

Sticky posts from a category

WP Recent Posts From Category

Displays recent posts from selected category by generating a shortcode that can be used in widgets, posts and pages.

By Daniele De Santis

Install Now

More Details

 (5)

2,000+ Active Installs

Last Updated: 4 weeks ago

✓ Compatible with your version of WordPress

Make any WordPress element a sticky while scrolling up and down the page

Sticky Menu (or Anything!) on Scroll

Sticky Menu (Or Anything!) On Scroll will let you choose any element on your page that will be "sticky" at the top once you scroll down.

By Mark Senff

Installed

More Details

 (45)

10,000+ Active Installs

Last Updated: 4 months ago

Untested with your version of WordPress

Notifications

It is important to keep all of your site's users and visitors informed and engaged. Default WordPress setting will dictate how often administrators receive notifications from the site. Subscribers of your site should be notified when pages, posts, and media is added or updated. Regular notifications are a great way to make users feel like they are involved but understand they site visitors are not signing up to be harassed by a barrage of notifications from your site.

By default, WordPress sends notifications of:

- New Comment / Comment Awaiting Moderation
- New Trackback
- New Pingback
- Lost Password (For Admin)
- New User Registration (For Admin)

WordPress Discussion Settings

Default WordPress notification can be modified under Discussion Settings.

Default Article Settings: Pingbacks, Trackbacks, and Comments are displayed by default if you want notifications or comments to show in the bottom section of your posts.

Other Comment Settings: Additional comment settings can be included to help moderate content posted on your web site by visitor. One of these optional settings is to require commenters to include an email address with their comment. Even though commenters do not have to leave their REAL email – it may deter lazier folks and bots from leaving useless comments. You can force those who want to interact with you by commenting on your posts or reading private posts and pages to register for your site. Additionally, content that is created for certain time periods can be given expiration dates, which limits users' ability to comment after an expiration date.

Email Me Whenever: As the content owner, you can be notified by email whenever there is activity on the site.

Before a Comment Appears: As the content owner you are in control of the activity on the site. You may want user comments available for publishing to site when they click enter, or you may wish to filter comments before they can be posted.

Online Notifcations

Your site should have the ability to alert users if when something happens with the site that affect them. WordPress currently controls visitor notification via plugins.

Email Notifications SMS Notifications	Push Notifications to iOS Devices Push Notifications Android Devices	Notification Bars	Contact Forms

Email and SMSNotifications: Site users and visitors are already comfortable with receiving online notifications, so they are expecting to hear from you too when they subscribed to your site. Most plugins allow email filtering based on user role.

SMS (text) Notifications: Reaching out and updating users via text message is a relatively new and instant method to connect with users. SMS or text messages should really be used in moderation considering this is considered to be a more personal avenue of communication than email. Users are more likely to feel SPAMMED from too many messages sent via text.

Real-Time Push Notifications to iOS/Android Devices: Mobile devices are now the most common requestors of web-based content. Capitalizing on their usefulness will go far in helping you to achieve your user-engagement goals. Most push notification plugins are not completely free. Most require site owners to sign up for a subscription of some sort. Most of the push notification plugins reviewed offered geo-targeted push notifications, scheduling push notifications, visitor locations, visual heatmaps, can generate short-URLs, and real-time analytics.

On Screen Notification Bars: Require the user to visit the site to see the notification which in most plugins can reside in the header, footer, left side or the right side of your site.

Contact Forms: Allows site visitors to engage with the site owner by having the ability to send an email from your site.

Modifying WordPress Post Names (Permalinks)

The permalink is the URL the user sees in their browser address bar. It is made from the name of the post or page. URL addresses are all lower-case and cannot contain spaces, so spaces are replaced by dashes.

To edit the Permalink:

STEP 1. Change the name in the text box following the URL protocol of no spaces or capital letters.

STEP 2. Click the **OK** button. The old permalink in replaced by the new one.

STEP 3. Click the **Update** button to save these changes.

Multipage Posts

Placing <!--nextpage--> in text view in the location where you want the content to split.

If this action does not split your content, go one step further:

Place <?php wp_link_pages(); ?> in the single.php file inside the WordPress loop.

STEP 1.   Hover over the **Appearance** link in the left main menu and then click the **Editor** link from the submenu.

Result: The edit page with the links to the site templates displays.

STEP 2.   Click on the **Single Post** link in the Templates menu.

STEP 3.   Locate the WordPress Loop. Paste (ctrl+v) the next page code within the loop.

<?php wp_link_pages(); ?>

STEP 4.   Click on the **Update File** button to save your changes. Text the functionality.

Deleting and Restoring Deleted Posts

Creating and maintaining a WordPress web site is an on-going process with posts, pages and comments constantly being added and deleted from the site, thus the database. When a post, page or comment is deleted it is moved to the trash folder. The trash folder is visible when view the all pages, all posts, and all comments pages.

Open the **post or page** you want to delete.

Click on the **Move to Trash** link.

Result: A notification displays and the Trash folder now has 1 file.

To remove a post or a page from the trash:

First, answer the following:

1. How many posts are in the Trash folder?
2. Press the **Empty Trash** button the permanently delete the posts in the Trash.
3. The title of the post in the trash.

Next:

STEP 1. Click on the post title you want to restore.

STEP 2. Click on the **Restore** link to restore the post to the all posts area.

STEP 3. Click on the **Delete Permanently** to trash it for real and for good.

Result: The post is restored to the **All Posts** listing.

CATEGORIES

Organize Your Posts with Categories

Post Categories Section

By default, WordPress themes come with an **Uncategorized** category. You will learn how to create and configure the full Categories list in Chapter 8: *Site Organization*.

A category can easily be created from the Posts screen:

STEP 1. Click the **+ Add New Category** link.

Result: A text box will appear.

STEP 2. Type in the new Category Title.

STEP 3. Click the **Add New Category** button. Your new Category will now appear checked by default in the All Categories List.

IMAGE MANAGEMENT

WordPress Media Settings

The images used in your posts, pages, and galleries are controlled in the media section. WordPress allows you to make changes to the dimensions of images. Images can still be sized at the time of insert.

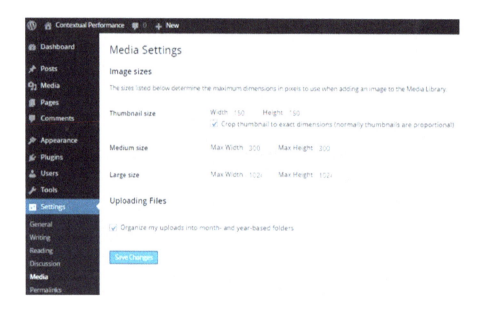

Image Sizes

Image sizes

The sizes listed below determine the maximum dimensions in pixels to use when adding an image to the Media Library.

Working with Images

WordPress functionality allows for the scaling, cropping, rotating, and horizontal and vertical flipping of images in the default install.

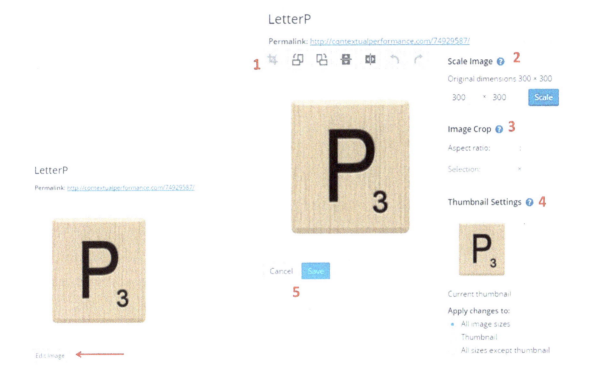

STEP 1. **Rotating and Flipping Images:** WordPress allows for the rotating and flipping (counter-clockwise, clockwise, flip vertically, and flip horizontally) of images in the Media Library.

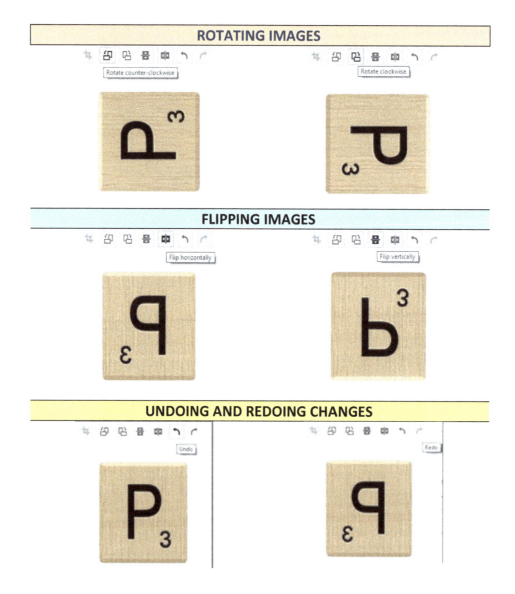

STEP 2.   **Scaling (Resizing) Images:** WordPress allows for the resizing of images within the Media Library by typing in the desired length and/or width of the image.

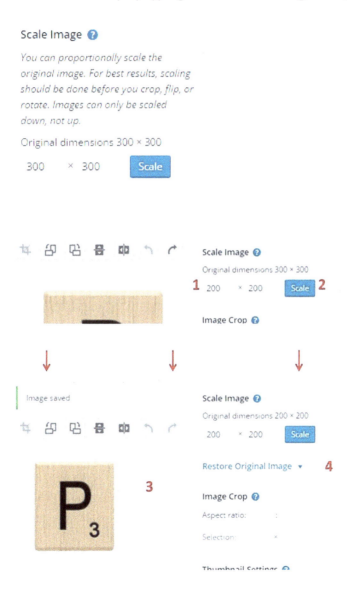

STEP 1.   Type in the height and/or width desired.

STEP 2.   Click on the **Scale** button

Result: The newly scaled image is displayed.

STEP 3.   Review your changes.

STEP 4.   To reverse the scaling, click on the **Restore** dropdown arrow and click on the **Restore Image** button.

Cropping an Image: WordPress allows the cropping of images in the Media Library by dragging a crop area and by using aspect ratios.

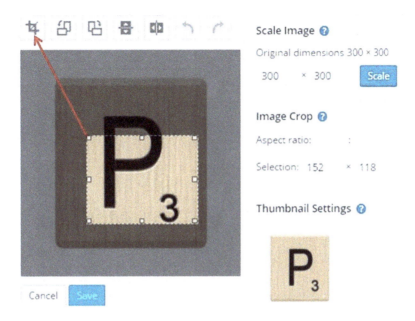

STEP 1.   Drag an area of the image you want cropped out of the original image.

STEP 2.   Click on the **Crop** button to complete the crop.

Result: The newly cropped image is displayed.

STEP 3.   Review your changes. To reverse the crop, click on the **Undo** button. To save
           your changes, click on the **Save** button.

Image Compression

Media in the form of music, videos, and images are the main culprits of slow sites. Unfortunately, music and videos cannot be compressed for increased site optimization easily but images can. Many images sizes can be made smaller without any visual loss of quality.

First, let's take a look at the most common image types:

	USE	TYPE	COLORS	SPECIALITY	COMPRESSION	SIZE
JPEG/JPG Joint Photographic Experts Group	Photograph	Raster	24-Bit	Resolution of Pixels	Lossy	Largest
GIF	Simple Graphic	Raster	256 Pixels	Fully opaque or transparent pixels	Lossless	Smallest
PNG Portable Network Graphic	Complex Graphic	Raster	Millions of Pixels	Animation 8-Bit Transparency Layers	Lossless	

A **JPG** is an example of a *lossy* image. Photographs can undergo substantial optimization. The removal of data from the pixels of the photograph to make the file size smaller is called **Lossy** compression. Lossy compression is a permanent removal of color and thus the photograph cannot be restored back to its original state.

A **GIF** is a very *small* file. Compression of a gif is in most cases impossible because it is as small as it will get even after compression.

A **PNG** is another example of a *lossless* image. A PNG supports millions of colors and taut excellent quality It supports full transparency, the ability to set the opacity of an element within images from zero (invisible) to 100 (full visibility). Lossless compression temporarily removes some of the data from the image that can be restored at any time.

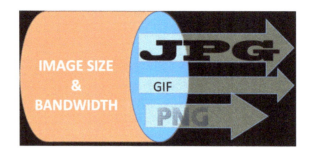

What is image compression?

Compression is the act of reducing the file size of an image by stripping out unneeded and redundant (identical) file information. Images undergo different changes when undergoing compression to make them smaller.

How will compressing my site images help my site?

The average mature web site could have thousands of images. Many times a logo, header image(s), ads, post images, footer images text support images all on one screen. It is smart to be mindful of loading times for each and how visitors with slower Internet connection are experiencing your site. A high-speed connection is no longer a connection drawback for visitors, it is the competition for bandwidth. Whether on a traditional computer, laptop, or phone, people click away from sites that are slow to load. High conversion rates is the goal for any web site and a slow loading site due to uncompressed, heavy images will halt your success.

Using Compression Plugins

Unless you are very familiar with graphics, there is no reason for you to know anything about the lossiness, weight, transparency, etc. and in this case you don't have to. You can use plugins design to compress images used on WordPress sites. There are free and for pay plugins to accomplish your compression goals.

Read the small print:
With a free account you can compress roughly 100 images each month.

 Compress JPEG & PNG images

Speed up your website. Optimize your JPEG and PNG images automatically with TinyPNG.

By: TinyPNG.

 (56)

40,000+ active installs

←——→

Last Updated: 2 weeks ago

Compatible up to: 4.4.1

Impressive:
Over 200K Active Installs and update 2 weeks ago.

 EWWW Image Optimizer

Reduce file sizes for images in WordPress including NextGEN, GRAND FlAGallery and more using lossless/lossy methods and image format conversion.

By: nosilver4u.

 (219)

200,000+ active installs

←——→

Last Updated: 2 weeks ago

Compatible up to: 4.4.1

CHAPTER TWO: ENGAEMENT STRATEGIES

In this chapter you will learn website engagement techniques. This chapter introduces you to the best practices of designing for the web to give the user the experience of being connected to your content.

In this chapter, you will:

- Learn how to build a strong engagement strategy
- Learn how to incorporate notifications into your engagement strategy
- Learn how to manage AVATARS
- Learn how to link authors to their posts

The first step in creating an engaging site is to understand how your users expect to interact with your content. Engagement extends beyond driving users to your site. Once they have landed on your content, what is your plan to engage them and more importantly, make them want to return? In this chapter, you are provided with the tools for engaging users through WordPress built-in functionality, good web design, and plugins. Later in the book we will discuss user centered design (UCD) and user experience (UX) in detail.

DEVELOPING YOUR WEB SITE ENGAGEMENT STRATEGY

When developing the strategy, there are several questions you should keep in mind:

- **Who is your audience?**

    Children, young adults, teens, adults, grandparents

    Tech savvy, new to tech, the swipe generation (0-6 years)?

    Will they visit several times an hour or a day?

    Will you offer basic or advanced Searching?
    Are you going to interact with your visitors beyond general forms?

    Do you plan to blog, live chat, or deploy social widgets?

    Do you plan to robustly moderate comments left on your posts?

- **How will you personalize their experience with your content?**

    Will you utilize polling?

    Will they upload and share their content?

    Will you allow for Customer Reviews and Feedback?

It is advisable to dig into designing for the web articles and tutorials when developing your site strategy.

Defining Your Site's Engagement Strategy

Defining an engagement strategy for your site is a very personal and individual endeavor. Most of the questions you need to answer will be unique. You should at a minimum be concerned with:

- How many visitors you have?

- How long they stay?

- How often they return?

This will require digging into the analytics of your site to see how many pages they visited and how long they stayed on each.

Setting Engagement Goals

Set expectations for the users of your site in the forms of engagement goals. Later in the chapter, we will review available engagement plugins available for WordPress and how to use the information you'll receive from them. It is not enough to know the jargon or activate the plugins without a plan that includes goals and expectations.

What do you want from your users?	What do you want to do for them?	Are you a proprietor of information or a seller of goods and services?

Once you clarify why users should visit your site and what you want them to do once they get there it will allow you to craft goals for which you later measure and track.

Engagement Strategy Elements

There are many different elements that can be used to engage users on your site. You can use one engagement application that encompasses several tools or you can choose and deploy individual plugins. It will be up to you to find the mix of these elements that work best to accomplish your web site goals. You do have web site goals, don't you? If not, I would make some before moving on.

Adding a Blog as a Tool of Engagement

A great addition to a traditional site to further engage users is the addition of a blog of timely and appropriate posts to accompany static information. Be aware there is a lot more work that goes into a live site than on a traditional (static web pages) one.

MODERATION IS THE KEY	Are you SPAMMING?	Are you Absent?
POST INFORMATION	Audience	Reading Level
	Relevance	Up-to-Date
IMAGES	Relevance	Engaging
RESPONSES	Moderation of Comments	Timely Responses

When using posts as a tool of engagement you want to be sure to keep your post relevant and regular. Make decisions on how often you can keep content refreshed.

This strategy can work against you if you are not **all-in**. Not only do you have to make the time and resource commitment to keep new content on the site you will also have to moderate comments and respond to comments in a timely manner.

Using Plugins as a Form of Engagement

There are plugins to ease the work with posts. Useful scheduling posts plugins can:
Schedule new post publish
- Unpublish dates
- Schedule a release of old posts
- Schedule stickiness
- Open and close a post for comments

U2USERS [You and Users]
U2CONTRIBUTORS [You and Contributors]
USERS2U [Users and You]
USER2USER [Site Users with One Another]

U2USERS	Membership	User Registration	Events	Calendar	Maps	Tour
Celebration Card Creator		Quality Control Check	Recipes	SEO	Graphs	Tables
Live Chat	Social Analytics	Products Search	Newsletter	Page/Post Publication/Expiration		
	Contact Builder	Tattoo Designer		Import/Export Management		
Real-Time Notifications		Site Map Generator	Virtual Try-On [Contacts, Jewelry, Eyewear]			
USERS2U		Digital Downloads	Appointment & Venue Management			
Food Ordering		Testimonials	Donations & Pledges			
U2CONTRIBUTORS		Visual Composer	Email Composers Forms			
User Management		Polling	Product Voting & Notifications			
USER2USER		Profile Management	Social Status			
Upload and Share						

When Schedule Post Publish is entered into the search bar in the Plugin Directory of the Codex (wordpress.org), 312 results were found.

Polls

Having users engage in on-page polls has proven to be a quick, fun way to engage users while gathering information. A rule of thumb is to keep the poll to just a couple of short questions.

Customer Reviews and Feedback

All of the major retail sites actively engage users for reviews and you should too. There is a lot of information that can be garnered from hearing from your users. Yes, some will use it as a space to gripe, but there will be those that want to tell you about a positive experience and you want to be in a position to receive it.

Charts and Graphs

Using images to give visual context to text is a given, but users also appreciate when authors provide charts and graphs to give visual context to facts, figures, and statistics.

Advanced Site Search

Making it easy to find information on your site could be as easy as placing search bars in easy to locate areas around your site. Fortunately, most WordPress themes come with search capability built in. Make sure the functionality is turned on and accessible.

Adding advance search capabilities to your site will extend search possibilities, giving your users more control to find the information they are looking for.

Relevant Technology

Staying abreast of popular technology, applications, etc. should definitely be in your arsenal of engagement tools. The tools you use on your site should align with the technical levels and experience your audience.

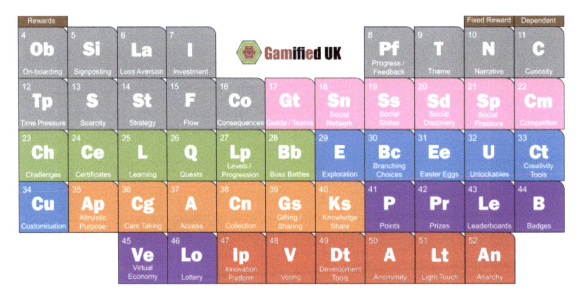

https://www.gamified.uk/user-types/gamification-mechanics-elements/

Two popular engagement tools are Gamification and sharable content. Chapter 7 is dedicated to how to make your site social. Gamification is relatively new and at this time there are only 13 search results when Gamification is entered into the WordPress.org plugin search bar.

Forms

Forms are used as a form of *user engagement*. Millions of forms are submitted via the web daily, so understanding and mastering the role forms play in the success of your site is crucial. Most Web sites use forms to elicit feedback from their users. The most common type of form is the contact form., but there are many other types of forms that are often overlooked because of common and simplistic nature of their use.

Registration			
Subscription			Map & Directions
	Contact		Audio/Video
	Feedback	Order	
	Surveys	Event Registration	SMS

Make sure the plugin you choose is compatible to the version of WordPress you have installed. If not you will receive an error message.

Registration Forms: Allowing users the convenience of registering online is a great form of engagement that has been on the web for years and users are quite comfortable with using them. Making a registration form as simple as possible is the key, don't bombard them with a lot of hoops to jump through. You can gather more specific information about the user once registration is complete.

Subscription Forms: Filling out forms to join a newsletter is another that is found commonly on the web. I would implore you to take the time to find out how often your users are comfortable with receiving information as to not make them fill SPAMMED. Also, make sure there is an easy way for users to unsubscribe.

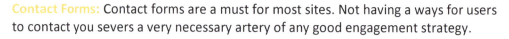

Contact Forms: Contact forms are a must for most sites. Not having a ways for users to contact you severs a very necessary artery of any good engagement strategy.

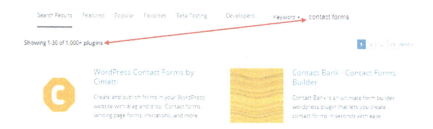

Feedback Forms: Eliciting feedback on site information, products, posts, etc. is a great way for users to feel invested in the information on the site. Studies have shown, when users feel invested they are more likey to return.

Surveys: Gathering information for measurable feedback via surveys is a tricky undertaking, but if done correctly, it can be a very effective way of eliciting feedback on particular topics of interest. The trick here is balance. It has been shown that surveys that are too long or complicated are abandoned and never completed. Experts advise to keep online surveys as short as possible, break questions up into manageable chunks, and guide users through the survey giving context clues as to when they are as they progress through the survey.

Order Forms: Having a straightforward way for users to complete the ordering process directly affects the success of getting your product off of your shelves and into the purchasers hand. Take great care to make this process as painless as possible for the user. At a minimum order forms should be easy to read and understand, policies should be clearly stated, and the payment gateway/checkout options used should work seamlessly to avoid looking clunky or illegitamate.

Event Registration Forms: Sites that advertise and book events of any size or type need to deploy the right event registration form to get the job done. Tracking attendant preferences, information, and decisions are an important part of event registration not directly apparent on the form itself. When registering attendants to events make sure you are using the right template or plugin for the job.

Maps and Directions: Online and mobile maps have undoubtedly revolutionized how we move about the world and not having a map to your physical environment equals webmaster malpractice. There are many options for charting directions on your site and I will leave the specifics up to you----but, as you can clearly see, some flavor of Google Maps dominates the first page of map direction results in the WordPress Plugin Directory.

Related Content: Adding relevant content such as e-newsletter, if done with care will give your content a feeling of well-roundedness. Placing relevant video even if you are not the author is a smart move. YouTube, Vimeo, and other non-proprietary videos engage users who prefer to watch instead of read. The most valuable but resource consuming is offering a live chat on your site. This tool offers users the ability to engage instantly.

Staying Connected: The conversation with your site users should expand beyond responding to comments. After users register to receive notifications you should reward them by having a robust notification system. Within the notification remember to keep the conversation going by asking engaging questions or by rewarding them for their participation with an appropriate reward.

Functionality Plugins

WordPress has made it really easy for non-developers to used complex pieces of code very easily on their site. The more difficult part about using plugins extending the functionality, that is learning how to configure the plugin to do what you want it to do. Going into the plugin settings is configuring the plugin.

Some configurations will be pretty straight-forward, only taking a couple of minutes and there are those that will take thought, planning, and time to get them just right. It is also at configuration that will see whether the functionality you require comes with the free version or whether the plugin author offers "the good stuff" in a paid or subscription version of the plugin.

Up to this point you have saved a lot of money using WordPress, I advise spending the money necessary of themes and plugins to make your site a premium experience.

POST SCREEN OPTIONS

The quality and speed in which you are able to create content for your web site is important. Setting of the posts and pages screens to best reflect your workflow is not something you should overlook. Using the drag and drop interface provided by WordPress makes it easy to set up your workspace in a way that maximizes productivity by placing on the screen options you use in places where they are most accessible while removing those that you rarely use at all.

By default, the following screen options are selected.

Additional Screen Options: These options allow you to add additional functionality and elements to your posts. Screen options will vary based on the theme installed.

1. **Excerpt:** This is an optional summary or description of a post. WordPress generates an excerpt automatically by selecting the first 55 words of the post. You will need to use the excerpt template tag. Plugins are available to more easily administer excerpts.

2. **Send Trackbacks:** Trackbacks are a way to notify legacy blog systems that you have links in your posts to their posts.

3. **Custom Fields:** These are used to add additional meta-data to your post. They must be placed in name (key)/value pairs. Keys can be reused with different values, but the value is what shows in the meta-data listing. You will need to use the excerpt template tag. Plugins are available for easier administration of custom fields.

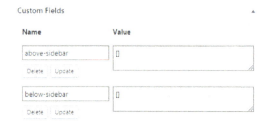

4. **Discussion:** Use checkmarks to determine whether you allow comments, trackbacks, or pingbacks for your post. To remove this functionality from posts, remove the checkmark from the checkboxes.

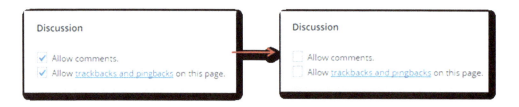

5. **Slug:** A slug is a URL-friendly version of the post or page title. It is also found on the categories screen, used when creating post categories.

6. **Author:** To choose the author of the post. Click dropdown arrow and Click the user who will be credited as the author of the post.

Drag-and-Drop Widgets

Let's drag and drop your homepage.

STEP 1.   Hover over the **Quick Draft** widget.
STEP 2.   Hold the left mouse down until it turns into a 4-headed arrow.

STEP 3.   Move your mouse to another area on the page and let go of the left mouse button.

AUTHORS AND THEIR POSTS

Creating a more robust experience for your users and post authors gives your site a professional experience. Making it easy to follow certain authors and providing a link to a great-looking author page.

Bios and Author Pages

Robust author bios at the end of your site's posts show that your authors are reputable authors that are worthy of the read. In most cases, plugins take a snippet of text from the author's bio page and places it at the end of their posts. There are several places you can place and author's name or a snippet of their information with a link that will take the user to the full bio.

Most plugins will place author names, avatars, or bio snippets in:

- Tag clouds
- Widgets
- Menus

ernwpthemes.com | designrshub.com | blogcastfm.com

MEASURING ENGAGEMENT

So, a reasonable question is: Is my engagement strategy working? As I was researching engagement, I read many, many articles and lots of comments. One that stuck with me said, "I've tried all of these things, and the only person who visits my site is me". My heart sunk for him, mainly because I have been in his place. Having an awesome web site and a well-crafted engagement strategy does not guarantee visitors. The web is not that different than any other business endeavor. The truth is some ideas and work bear fruit and others just don't. It is my hope that you will catch lightening in your bottle and make it work!

The factors you choose to measure and track should be determined by your web sites goals and aligned with its strategies. Let's explore how you will measure your engagement endeavors using Engagement rating and tracking. Your engagement results and metrics should answer the questions posed when you formed your goals.

The chart below gives an idea of how to connect the factors that make-up your goals to what you are measuring. It is from there you can track your results, draw conclusions as to the accomplishment of your set engagement goals. Specialists in the area of web site engagement agree: activities/factors should be the focus when measuring and tracking the user engagement of your site. Here's what they're saying:

- ConvinceAndConvert.com calculates engagement rates by adding up the instance of each of the activities (factors) defined in your goals and dividing that number by your web sites total unique daily.

- **Filament.io's** approach is less mathematical. They advise web site owners to isolate important activities (factors), track them over time, establish a baseline, and figure out how you can tweak your site to get the results you seek.

- **AnalyticsDemystified.com** also recommends using active (activities/factors) to measure and rate the engagement of your visitors.

FACTORS	METRICS	TRACKING
	Web site Traffic	Recognizing Patterns
	Pageviews	Behaviors
Web Analytics	Average Time on Page	Duration
	Session Duration	Scroll Depth
	Bounces	Registration/New Users
Blog Email/SMS Notifications Site Search	Internal links clicked	Click Depth
Online Forms	Form Submissions	Feedback
Sharable Content	Shares	Share Rate
Polls	Votes	Poll Rate
Relevant Content	YouTube, Vimeo, and other Non-Proprietary Videos	Video Play Rate
Newsletter	Sign-Ups	Interaction
Customer Reviews	Testimonials	Loyalty Brand

CHAPTER THREE: WORKING WITH DYNAMIC CONTENT

> *This chapter introduces you to the WordPress shortcodes. The ability to create an item and reuse it throughout the site. Shortcodes also gives you the ability to make a change to content while the changes flow to every other instance of that content in your site.*

In this chapter, you will:

- Learn about shortcodes
- Learn about WordPress built-in shortcodes
- Learn about shortcode-rich themes
- Learn about premium shortcode plugins

Shortcodes are reusable content that are given names that can be used throughout your site. Shortcodes names are surrounded by brackets and placed in the design page of a post or a page. Shortcodes are often accompanied by attributes that allow you to control its functionality.

[ShortcodeName]	Shortcode name in brackets
[ShortcodeName attribute]	Shortcode name - each attribute is separated by a space
[[ShortcodeName]]	To show the shortcode name without launching the shortcode use double-brackets
[ShortcodeName]...[/ShortcodeName]	Some shortcodes need to be wrapped around the functionality

There are a number of ways to find shortcodes for your site. Wordpress offers several built-in shortcodes, premium themes usually come with shortcodes built into the theme, and finally you can purchase shortcode bundles from their developers.

WORDPRESS BUILT-IN SHORTCODES

Wordpress has shortcodes that are downloaded with the installation. Most of the following shortcodes can be found in the wp-includes folder.

The [audio] shortcode places audio files into posts and pages.

Attribute	Attribute Properties
src	[audio src="audio-source.mp3"]
autoplay	autoplay="on/off"
loop	loop="on/off"
preload	preload ="none/auto/metadata Defaults is "none"

The [caption] shortcode allow caption to content or an image.

Attribute	Attribute Properties
[caption]<image> and/or text[/caption]	
Id	Id="css"
class	class="css"
align	align="alignnone/aligncenter/alignright/alignleft"
width	width="width="#" height="#""

The [embed] shortcode has an opening and closing tag and allows for the embedding of video and other object into posts and pages.

Attribute	Attribute Properties
[embed width="123" height="456"]http://www.youtube.com/watch?v=dQw4w9WgXcQ[/embed]	
width	width="#"
height	height="#"

The [gallery] shortcode places galleries of the attached images into your posts and pages.

Attribute	Attribute Properties
order	order="ASC/DESC"
columns	columns="#"
id	id="#"
size	size="thumbnail/medium/large/full"
link	link="file/none"

The [playlist] shortcode places a set of audio files into your posts and pages.

Attribute	Attribute Properties
type	type="audio/video" The default is audio.
order	order "ASC/DESC" Ascending or Descending The default is ascending.
Orderby	orderby="menu_oder ID"
id	id= "$post ? $post->ID : 0"
include	include=""
exclude	exclude=""
style	style="light/dark" The default is light.
Tracklist	tracklist="true/false" True is show /Hide is false The default is true.
tracknumbers	tracknumbers="true/false" True is show /Hide is false The default is true.
images	images="true/false" True is show /Hide is false The default is true.
artists	artists="true/false" True is show /Hide is false The default is true.

The [video] shortcode places a set of video files into your posts and pages.

Attribute	Attribute Properties
src	src="name.extension"
poster	poster="image/none"
loop	loop="on/off"
autoplay	autoplay="on/off"
preload	preload="metadata/none/auto"
width	width="#"
height	height="#"

SHORTCODES IN THE DASHBOARD

Shortcodes are normally found on the formatting toolbar on posts and pages. These shortcodes show up on the formatting toolbar under a *specialized icon, depending on the template*.

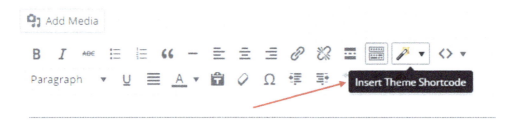

Some themes place individual icons on the formatting toolbar. In this theme the

- **Insert Columns**

- **Insert Portfolio**

- **Insert Modules, and**

- **Insert ContactForm** are all accessible from the formatting toolbar.

WORDPRESS.ORG SHORTCODES PLUGINS

Wordpress.org offers many great shortcodes by way of plugins.

Current Year and Copyright Shortcodes

Provides Shortcodes to display the Current Year and/or a Copyright symbol.

By: David Gewirtz

★★★★★ (5)

3,000+ active installs

Last Updated: 5 months ago

Compatible up to: 4.3.3

Column Shortcodes

Adds shortcodes to easily create columns in your posts or pages.

By: Codepress, Tobias Schutter, and David Mosterd

★★★★★ (70)

100,000+ active installs

Last Updated: 1 year ago

Compatible up to: 4.1.10

PREMIUM SHORTCODES

Premium shortcode plugins can be purchased from developers or affiliates for as low as $5.00, the high end could be as much as $30.00.

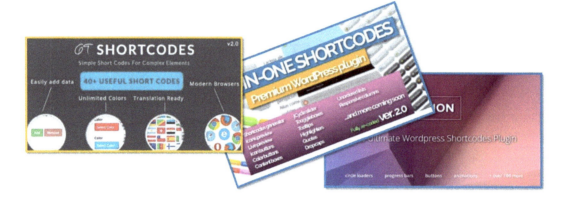

When premium shortcodes is entered into the Google search box the first 6 hits seemed to be promising sources:

WordPress › Shortcodes Ultimate « WordPress Plugins
https://**wordpress**.org/plugins/**shortcodes**-ultimate/ ▼ WordPress ▼
Turn your free theme to **premium** in just a few clicks. Using **Shortcodes** UI
can quickly and easily retrieve **premium** themes features and display it on
WordPress › Shortcodes Ultimate - Installation - FAQ - Changelog

5 Awesome Free WordPress Shortcode Plugins - WPM
https://**premium**.wpmudev.org/.../5-awesome-free-**wordpress**-shortc
Jul 26, 2014 - **WordPress** introduced the **shortcode** API with the release of
2.5 ... There are also **premium** add-ons – extra **shortcodes** (15+ extra ...

25 Awesome Shortcodes & Page Builder Plugins For ...
www.wpexplorer.com › Blog › WordPress Plugins ▼
May 11, 2014 - Check out these 25 best free and **premium WordPress** sho
and page builders to help make your WordPress website development ...

Vision - Wordpress Shortcodes Plugin - CodeCanyon
codecanyon.net/item/vision-**wordpress**-**shortcodes**-plugin/3372371
★★★★☆ Rating: 4.2 - 122 votes - $25.00 - In stock
Nov 9, 2012 - Complete List of Features: Gorgeous Design – Perfect for eve
Plugin installs in under 1 minute **Shortcodes** get added directly to your ...

Supreme Shortcodes | WordPress Plugin - WordPress .
codecanyon.net/item/supreme-**shortcodes**-**wordpress**-plugin/63407(
★★★★☆ Rating: 4.4 - 92 votes - $21.00 - In stock
Dec 11, 2013 - Supreme **Shortcodes** – version 0.2.7 available. Download no
Shortcodes makes your **WordPress** website beautiful! This plugin .

Blog - Premium WordPress plugins and themes
https://lizatom.com/blog/ ▼
This Shortcodes Master add-on brings you a beautiful set animated service
Shortcodes Master – **Premium WordPress shortcodes** plugin, keep your .

Just as with the plugins we have encountered in the past, the author may offer some functionality of their plugin at no cost, but to have access to all of the (in this case) shortcodes, you will have to upgrade to the PRO version.

SHORTCODES WITH PREMIUM THEMES

One of the things that make premium themes worth the money is the bells and whistles they have built in. It is not unusual to have on average 20 premium shortcodes. There are even plugins that allow you with a bit of work to create your own custom shortcodes.

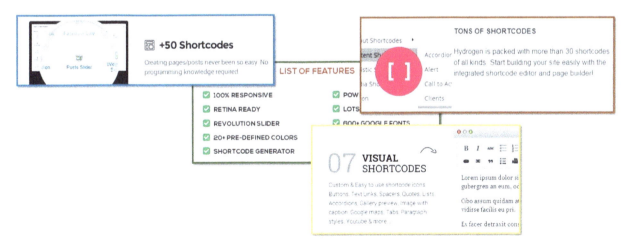

Here is a partial list of all of the items you can create with shortcodes:

Columns	Visual Columns	Tables	Tabs	Accordion
Error Box	Success Box	Info Box	Content Boxes	Labels
Pricing Boxes	Callout Box	Animation	Container	Tooltips
Divider Dashed	Divider Solid	Dividers	DivClear	Custom Styling
Progress - Circular	Progress – Vertical	Counters	Bar Charts	Alerts
Weather	Login/Out Button	Buttons	Google Charts	Flipboard
Google Maps	Image Zoom	Portfolios	Staff Bios	Picture Frames
Ordered List	DropCaps	Quotes	Blockquotes	Pull Quotes
Unordered List	LineBreak	Highlighting	Abbreviations	Push Menu
Lists	Read More Button	Page Siblings	Related Posts	Grids
Social Icons	Facebook Embed Posts	Facebook Like	Digg Button	Follow Me
LinkedIn	Google+1	Flattr	Tumbler Button	Testimonials
Sharing Buttons	Custom URLs	Overlay	Image Icons	Bitcoin

SHORTCODES IN WIDGETS

WordPress widgets were originally created to provide a simple and easy-to-use way of giving design and structure control of the WordPress theme to the user. The great thing about widgets is that you can drag and drop them into your sidebars or any widget ready areas of your web site. This allows great flexibility to plugin and theme developers. They can add functionality into their products and let users decide when and where to use that functionality without messing with code.

What is a Widget?

What is a Widget?

A widget is no-code function block that provides functionality to sections of your web site. It is helpful to think of plugins and widgets as puzzle pieces that combine to create the site you desire. Widgets most commonly appear on the homepage in the header, sidebars, and footer sections of a WordPress site. Widgets include functionality such as a calendar, custom menus, advertising areas, search, social media, and news scrolls to name just a few. Some plugin functionalities are deployed through widgets or have a widget option.

Working with Widgets

To access the widget area:

STEP 1.   Hover over or click the **Appearance** link and then scroll over to and click **Widgets** in the Left Main Navigation menu.

Result: The Widget Area opens.

Configuring shortcodes in widgets is a process of expanding and adding functionality.

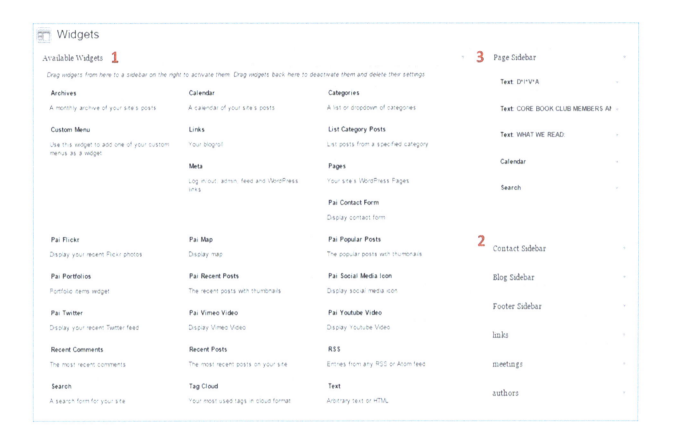

1. **Available Widgets for the Shortcodes**: Shortcode functionality that is available to place in widget areas either comes as a default with the theme or has been installed by the site owner. Available functionality is located on the left side of every widget area. The name of the widgets is the same as the plugin that was downloaded.

2. **Configuring the Shortcodes with Widgets**: Widgets are built by using and configuring the function code blocks from the left side of the widget area.

MAINTAINING SHORTCODES IN YOUR SITE

As any other functionality, shortcodes must be managed over time. It must be remembered that WordPress is a living install that is periodically updated. It is also up to the developer to update their plugins and keep them up-to-date. I recommend using shortcode plugins that are updated regularly.

Sometimes plugins are no longer supported or even worse run into fatal errors.

It may be nearly impossible to maintain all of the shortcodes that are in your posts and pages as it grows. There are many plugins to help you in your efforts to maintain the shortcodes used in your site. For instance, there are shortcodes that will help you locate and keep track of the shortcodes used in your post and pages.

Shortcodes In Use

List all the shortcodes that you have used within your content or custom fields, and find out exactly where they have been used.

By wittvb.

There are shortcodes that will hide and/or remove any broken shortcodes in your posts and pages throughout your site until you have a chance to go through and fix or delete them.

Remove Orphan Shortcodes

Quickly remove unused (orphan) shortcode tags from your content.

By: Meks.

Hide Broken Shortcodes

Prevent broken shortcodes from appearing in posts and pages.

By: Scott Reilly.

CHAPTER FOUR: A SITE FOR EVERYONE

This chapter covers what how to create a site that everyone on the web can enjoy. There is an introduction to the consortiums and web groups that develop and maintain the standards of the web.

In this chapter, you will:

- Introduced to leading web groups and consortiums
- Learn the elements of an accessible site
- Learn how to create a multilingual site

In this chapter we will review the structure, content, and media of a web site to ensure they meet or exceed the standards set forth for accessible web sites by web governance groups and consortiums.

ENSURING ACCESSIBILITY

Accessibility refers to principals and guidelines for personal, business, and government web sites that make web content such as text, images, and training materials more accessible to those with disabilities. The 508 Compliance Standards and Web Content Accessibility Guidelines WCAG are technical standards that outline the criteria for successfully developing web sites that ensure accessibility for all.

Some guidelines are in line with good web site design and you will comply without even realizing it. For instance, criteria for good navigation includes the ability of users navigating through a site know where they are and how to get to the information they are looking for. Users should also be able to understand site content, specifically as to the readability and characteristics of text and backgrounds.

WordPress is sensitive to these guidelines and the program has made it easier for web designers to adhere to them without coding. One example of this is that content and formatting are separated through the use of themes. The use of responsive themes allows web sites to meet guidelines suggesting that sites be adaptable from one device to another. Many of the other high priority compliance guidelines pertain to the creation of tables and forms. The WordPress Media Library offers ways for web site creators adhere to the guidelines to provide text alternatives for non-text elements without having to write code.

W3C

The World Wide Web Consortium (W3C) have since 1996, assembled working groups made up of individuals, commercial, educational, and governmental organizations who are interested in the growth of the Web by releasing HTML versions, standards, and specifications. Read more about this great organization at https://www.w3.org.

WCAG 2.0

Web Content Accessibility Guidelines (WCAG) 2.0, guidelines to make web site content more accessible was released in 2008 as an update to WCAG 1.0 released in 1999.

Elements of an Accessible Site and Plugins

Clean HTML: This is not a concern if you are not writing any additional HTML, CSS, or PHP for your site. The WordPress community works very hard to insure that the WordPress core is compliant with accessibility recommendations.

Real Accessability

Real Accessability plugin adds custom accessability such as font resizer, color inverse, black & white view and much more

By: realmediail.

Accessible External Text Links

I created this plugin to make external text links more accessible to people with disabilities

By: Myshock.

Keyboard Support: Users should be able to move around the web site without the use of a mouse.

Shutter Keys

This plugin adds keyboard navigation support with the left and right arrow keys to the Shutter Reloaded plugin.

By: ZetoTwo.

Text Alternatives for all Non-Text Content: WordPress encourages authors to fill in the following information for media elements in their sites.

Title: The name of the file at the time it was uploaded from your computer.

Caption: Captions appear below the media element (images & video) to comply with the 508 standard requiring synchronized captions and descriptions.

Accessible Video Library

Generates a library for your video information where you can upload caption files, include transcripts, and upload subtitles for other languages.

By: Joe Dolson.

Alt Text: The Alt Text describes the image and will show in its place if for some reason it does not render.

Description: The description is not visible to the user, but is read to the user by reader applications.

Update Image Tag Alt Attribute

This plugin updates the alt attribute for all images that have null alt attribute text with the attached post/page title or the file name

By: mauimarketing and Ben Lee.

A Style-Free Option: Using fonts that are not 'works of art' to the point they would not be easily recognized by screen reading applications.

ARIA (Accessible Rich Internet Application): Landmarks tell the assistive technology what it's reading, where they are on the page, and what to do next.

ResponsiveVoice Text To Speech

ResponsiveVoice the leading HTML5 text to speech synthesis solution, is now available for WordPress. Over 51 languages through 168 voices.

By: ResponsiveVoice.

Color Contrast: Colors should have a sharp contrast and not close in color and hue.

SOGO Accessibility

This plugin add accessibility menu to a WordPress Site, enable, black and white, contrasts, font size increase and more...

By: SOGO.

Seizure-Inducing Graphics: Graphics that blink relentless without the ability for the user to turn them off should not be used.

Time-Limits: Should be removed.

Creating a Multilingual Site

The WordPress' default language is English, but it has been translated into many other languages for the backend and language switching for web site visitors. A major part of accessibility is having your site available to as wide an audience as possible. You can download and install the WordPress application in your language using the instructions on the In Your Language page on the Wordpress.org (https://codex.wordpress.org/Installing_WordPress_in_Your_Language) site.

WPTB Language

With this plugin you can easily switch the WordPress language. It will download and install the language files from the WP Repository as needed.

By: webily.

xili-language

xili-language lets you create and manage multilingual WP site in several languages with yours or most famous localizable themes. Ready for CMS design.

By: Michel - xiligroup dev and MS dev.xiligroup.com.

You can also allow language switching for the users of the site using plugins as well a being built into premium themes.

CHAPTER FIVE: BEING SOCIAL

The social revolution has served to integrated Wordpress web sites with sharing sites. Utilizing sharing to integrated web site content is as important as the formulation of current content and sensible navigation.

In this chapter, you will:

- Learn to use third-party elements to author data
- Incorporate Facebook, Twitter, Instagram, and Pinterest on your site
- Work with email newsletters
- Learn the pros and cons of displaying ads to your site

In this chapter we will explore the option to enhance the social nature of your site. Web sites today are social vehicles. Adding social elements to your site is not optional. Users expect to be able to effortless share information from your site with others. The easier you make it for this to happen to the more satisfying the experience will be for your users as well as a marketing vehicle for you.

ANALYTICS FOR YOUR SITE

A very important ingredient of a successful web site is analytics. Analytics is the gathering and reporting of the interactions with your site. This should be addressed in your web site engagement plan. In your web site engagement plan you will create goals for your site. These engagement goals set the expectations for you and your user. Earlier forms of web site engagement were introduced as well as ideas for plugins that will elicit the information about your visitors you need to make informed decisions about the engagement elements that are working for you and which are not. As stated before, engaging users is an individual endeavor dependent on the goals for the site.

It is imperative to start the social endeavor of your site by understanding the profile of your visitors. Getting a baseline of who, when, and which pages your visitors are visiting is key to building a social strategy that will give you the results you are looking for. There are many plugins and 3rd-party applications that will gather the data needed.

Google Analytics

A popular analytics application through the years has been provided by Google. Many WordPress sites use Google Analytics and are satisfied with the statics they provide. There are 2 major steps to installing and configuring Google Analytics on your site.

First you will need to create a Google (Gmail) account for your WordPress site.

STEP 1.   Go to http://www.google.com/analytics/sign_up.html and create a Google account for the site. When creating a username for your Google account use a name that represents the domain name of your site.

For example, for the Thebitagroup.com site, creating the username TheBitaGroupWeb would work nicely.

STEP 2.   Log in to your new Gmail account.

STEP 3.   Click on the apps icon at the top of your Gmail page.

STEP 4.   Click on the **More** link until you get to the
           https://www.google.com/intl/en/about/products/ page. Scroll down to the
           Business section of the page and click on the **Analytics** link.

           Results: You will be taken to the Google Analytics home page
                   (http://www.google.com/analytics/sign_up.html).

STEP 5.   Click on the **SIGN IN** link.

STEP 6.   Choose **Google Analytics** from the drop-down menu.

           Result: You will be taken to the Google Analytics Dashboard.

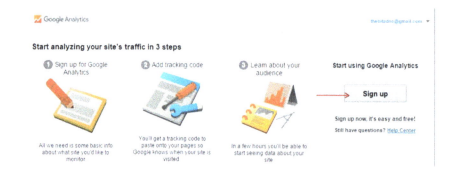

STEP 7.   Click on the **Sign up** button.

Result: You will be taken to the **New Account** page.

STEP 8.   **TRACKING METHOD:** Choose whether you are gathering analytics from a Web site or a Mobile app. In this case our goal is to gather analytics for our WordPress web site, so we will choose **Web site**.

STEP 9.   **SETTING UP YOUR ACCOUT:** Create an **Account Name** for your site.

STEP 10.   **SETTING UP YOUR PROPERTY:** Fill in the Web site Name, URL, Industry Category, and Reporting Time Zone.

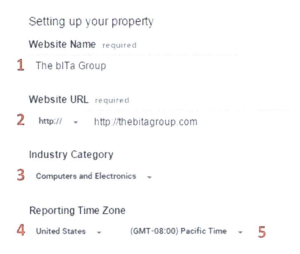

STEP 11.   Set up the **Data Sharing Settings**, Google will make recommendations.

STEP 12.   Click the **Get Tracking ID button** to complete this process.

STEP 13.   Click the **I ACCEPT** button to accept Google Analytics terms and conditions.

Result: You will be taken to the analytics dashboard for your site.

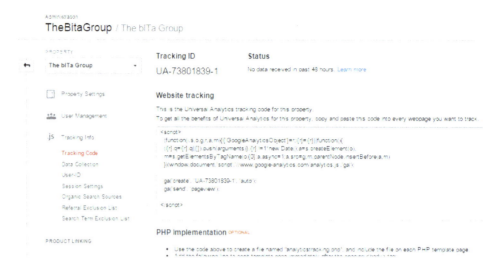

STEP 14. Open the NotePadd++ document where you are storing all of your site information (Creating a Web site using WordPress: The Beginners Guide) and place your Google Analytics Tracking ID and Code into it. You will need it to connect your site.

STEP 15. Before leaving this page go through the Settings on the left navigation and complete the setup for gathering and receiving results.

The second step in this process is to place the Tracking ID or Code into the WordPress installation.

This part is not difficult but can be accomplished a number of ways. It will up to you to determine which is best.

Within the Theme

> Most premium themes offer a place to Paste (ctrl+v) the information within their interface. Example: This theme allows for the tracking code to be places in the site' Theme Options.

STEP 1.   Click on **Theme Options**.

STEP 2.   Scroll down to Global Elements. Global elements are elements that affect the entire site.

GLOBAL ELEMENTS

STEP 3.   Scroll down until you see the **Google Analytics Tracking Code** text area
and Paste (ctrl+v) your tracking code there.

STEP 4.   Save the page.

Using a Plugin

There are many plugins that make adding analytic tracking information a point
and click process. WordPress.org has lots of good plugins for Google Analytics.
When Google Analytics is searched on in the Plugins section of the
WordPress.org web site there are 853 results are found.

Directly into the WordPress Code

To place the analytics tracking code directly into your wordpress installation:

STEP 1.   Click on the Dashboard link so that you will land on the right set of files in step 2.

The Editor link is contextual, meaning it will display the code (HTML/PHP) files for the area of the site you are on when the editor link is clicked.

STEP 2.   Click on the **Appearance** link and then click the **Editor** link.

STEP 3.   Click on the **Theme Header** (header.php) file in the right-hand menu on the Editor page.

Result: The Header file will display.

STEP 4.   Find the <body> tag in the header.php file.

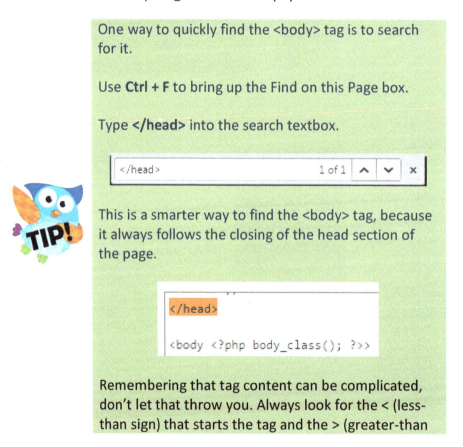

One way to quickly find the <body> tag is to search for it.

Use **Ctrl + F** to bring up the Find on this Page box.

Type **</head>** into the search textbox.

This is a smarter way to find the <body> tag, because it always follows the closing of the head section of the page.

Remembering that tag content can be complicated, don't let that throw you. Always look for the < (less-than sign) that starts the tag and the > (greater-than sign) that ends the tag.

```
<body <?php body_class(); ?>>
```

STEP 5.   Place your cursor to the right of the less-than sign of the <body> tag.

```
<body <?php body_class(); ?>>
```

STEP 6.   Move the cursor down a few lines by pressing the enter button twice. Paste (ctrl+v) the **Google Tracking** code there.

```
</head>

<body <?php body_class(); ?>>

<script>
  (function(i,s,o,g,r,a,m)
{i['GoogleAnalyticsObject']=r;i[r]=i[r]||function(){
  (i[r].q=i[r].q||[]).push(arguments)},i[r].l=1*new
Date();a=s.createElement(o),
  m=s.getElementsByTagName(o)
[0];a.async=1;a.src=g;m.parentNode.insertBefore(a,m)
  })(window,document,'script','//www.google-
analytics.com/analytics.js','ga');

  ga('create', 'UA-73801839-1', 'auto');
  ga('send', 'pageview');

</script>
```

STEP 7.   Scroll down and click the **Update File** button to save the Tracking Code in the theme's header file.

You're Good to Go!

PHP Implementation

Another way to add the Google Analytics Tracking Code into your WordPress site is by using the optional PHP Implementation. This code is found back on the Google Analytics dashboard below the Tracking Code. This option requires creating a new .php file and adding it to each of your template pages. Follow the directions carefully.

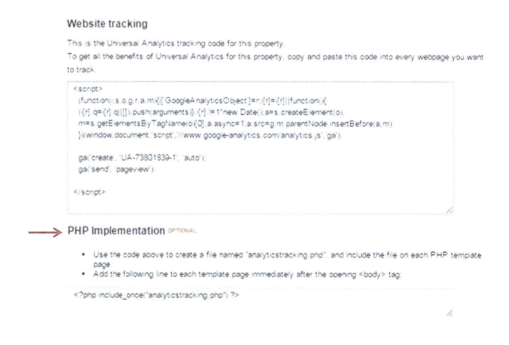

FACEBOOK INTEGRATION

A great social move for your web site is to create a Facebook page for your site. Integrating Facebook elements into your site take a bit of work on the front end, but will pay dividends in social exposure. Once you have created a separate Facebook profile for you site you can then move to integrating it into your site. There are 2 major steps to installing and configuring Facebook on your site.

First, you will need to create a Facebook page for your WordPress site.

To create a Facebook page for your site you must first have a personal Facebook page of your own. Once that is complete you will create a new page.

Log out of all Facebook profiles and go to the main login page. Click on the **Create a Page** link located under the signup button.

Go through the screens to complete the creation process. You will receive an email from Facebook to help you further develop your new Facebook page.

Get the most out of your Page for The BITA Group   Inbox x

Facebook <notification+knm54rxr@facebookmail.com> Unsubscribe
to me ▾

Next, you will add Facebook to your WordPress site using the Facebook Developers site, with a plugin, or within your theme.

Integrating Facebook using Facebook for Developers

STEP 1.   Login to your Facebook page.

STEP 2.   Go to https://developers.facebook.com/docs/plugins/page-plugin.

There are many different plugins available on this page.

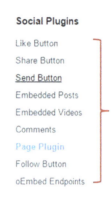

In this example will configure and install the **Page Plugin:**

STEP 3. Configure the Page Plugin settings to meet your needs, and then click the **Get Code** button.

> **Get Code**

STEP 4. Copy the **STEP 1 CODE** and Paste (ctrl+v) it in your theme's header.php file right after the <body> tag and click the **Update File** button to save your work.

Your Plugin Code   ×

1. Include the JavaScript SDK on your page once, ideally right after the opening <body> tag

STEP 1

```
<div id="fb-root"></div>
<script>(function(d, s, id) {
  var js, fjs = d.getElementsByTagName(s)[0];
  if (d.getElementById(id)) return;
  js = d.createElement(s); js.id = id;
  js.src = "//connect.facebook.net/en_US/sdk.js#xfbml=1&version=v2.5";
  fjs.parentNode.insertBefore(js, fjs);
}(document, 'script', 'facebook-jssdk'));</script>
```

```
</head>

<body <?php body_class(); ?>>

<div id="fb-root"></div>
<script>(function(d, s, id) {
  var js, fjs = d.getElementsByTagName(s)[0];
  if (d.getElementById(id)) return;
  js = d.createElement(s); js.id = id;
  js.src = "//connect.facebook.net/en_US/sdk.js#xfbml=1&version=v2.5";
  fjs.parentNode.insertBefore(js, fjs);
}(document, 'script', 'facebook-jssdk'));</script>
```

> **Update File**

STEP 5. Copy (ctrl+c) the **STEP 2 CODE** and Paste (ctrl+v) it in a post, page or widget to have your Facebook page to show on your site.

In this example, the STEP 2 CODE was placed in a text widget.

Result: Your Facebook page is displayed on your site. You can use this code over and over again.

Integrating Facebook using Plugins

Choose a plugin to integrate your Facebook page. Many plugins will ask you for your Facebook ID. Locating your Facebook ID:

STEP 1.   Click on the **Settings** link on your Facebook page.

STEP 2.   Click on **Page Info** in the left navigation.

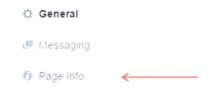

STEP 3.   Scroll to the bottom of the page to find Facebook Page ID.

Facebook Page ID   1967277236831685

TWITTER

Adding Twitter to your web site allows for the integration of tweets on your web site. It is recommended to use a plugin to accomplish this. First, you will need to create a Twitter account for your web site. Next, you need to find the plugin with the functionality you want for your site. When Twitter is entered into the Plugins section on WordPress.org, thousands of results were returned.

Twitter plugins range in installation complexity. At one time, if you wanted to display twitter on your web site you would have to create a twitter app then integrate it into your site. Today, developers have made it easier to integrate. It is advised to let the plugin instruct the installation and to stay clear of complicated Twitter plugins.

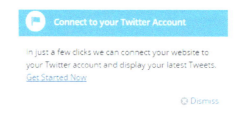

PINTREST

A popular photo sharing application is Pintrest. Adding Pinterest to your web site allows for the integration of boards, profile widgets, and follow buttons on your web site. It is recommended to use a plugin to accomplish this. First, you will need to create a Pinterest account for your web site. There are 2 major steps to installing and configuring Pintrest on your site.

For some Pinterest plugin you will need to generate a Pinterest Verification Code.

To Generate a Pintrest Verification Code:

STEP 1.   On your Pintrest main page, click on your **username**.

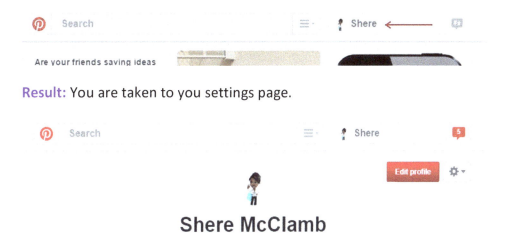

Result: You are taken to you settings page.

STEP 2.   Click on the **Gears** icon.

STEP 3.   Copy (ctrl+c) your Pintrest web site name from the URL bar.

STEP 4.   Click on the **Edit Setting** link in the drop down menu.

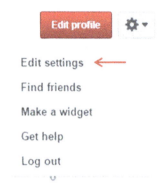

Result: You are taken to the **Accounts Basics** page.

Account Basics

STEP 5.   Scroll down to the **Profile** section.

Profile

STEP 6.   Paste (ctrl+v) you Pintrest web site URL into the **Web site** textbox and click on the **Confirm Web site** button.

Result: The **Confirm your web site** box appears.

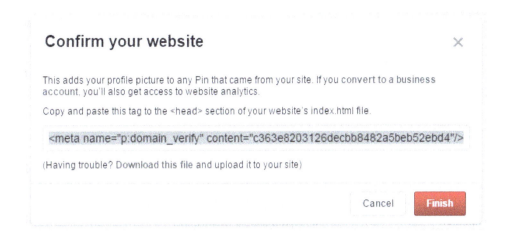

STEP 7.   Copy (ctrl+c) the code into your Notepadd++ file that contains your web site configuration information then click the **Finish** button.

The next step is to add the verification code to WordPress using a plugin.

First, you need to find the plugin with the functionality you want for your site.

When Pinterest is entered into the search textbox in the Plugins section on WordPress.org, 545 results were returned. Place the Pinterest boards, pin buttons, and Follow Me on Pinterest on your site in accordance to your engagement plan.

A popular way to keep your site users in the know is to email updates and periodic newsletters. Adding newsletter functionality to your web site allows subscribers to receive information in a time-effective way. The pricing and features for newsletters range from free to premium subscriptions with all the bells and whistles.

Newsletter Plugins Available on WordPress.org:

When **email newsletters** are typed into the plugins search box at WordPress.org, 515 results are displayed.
Review the choices and find the email newsletter plugin that best fits your engagement plan.

Top-Ranked Email Service Providers

If you already have an email service provider, check on their web site and in the plugins section of the WordPress.org site to see if there are any plugins available for integration with your site. There are WordPress plugins for many of the more popular email service providers in alphabetical order:

Benchmark Email

Available on the Benchmark web site.

Benchmark Email WordPress Plugin

The Benchmark Email WordPress Plugin includes a robust widget that lets you build an email list right from the pages of your WordPress site. Send formatted email versions of your blog posts, create custom signup forms and integrate your site with up to 5 separate Benchmark email accounts. Read More

Install Plugin

Available in the plugins section of the WordPress.org web site.

Benchmark Email Lite

Benchmark Email Lite lets you build an email list from your WordPress site, and easily send your subscribers email versions of your posts and pages.

By: bcAutomated, Sean Conklin, and Randy Sundberg.

★★★★☆ (3)
1,000+ active installs

Last Updated: 1 month ago
Compatible up to: 4.3.3

Contact Form 7 Benchmark Email Extension

Integrate your contact forms with the Benchmark Email service.

By: TheFitCoder.

☆☆☆☆☆ (0)
60+ active installs

Last Updated: 7 months ago
Compatible up to: 4.2.7

Constant Contact

Available in the plugins section of the WordPress.org web site.

Constant Contact for WordPress

Integrate Constant Contact into your website with this full-featured plugin.

By: Zack Katz and katzwebservices.

★★☆☆☆ (50)
10,000+ active installs

Last Updated: 6 months ago
Compatible up to: 4.3.3

iContact

IContact does not natively integrate with WordPress, but there are plugins written to integrate iContact.

MailChimp

The MailChimp web site offers an Integrations Directory (https://connect.mailchimp.com/search?q=wordpress). When the term WordPress is entered into the Integrations search bar, there are 62 integrations for WordPress.

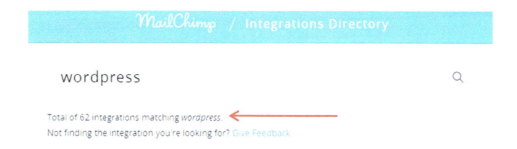

There are 430 MailChimp results in the plugins section on WordPress.org.

ADS ON YOUR SITE

Placing ads on your site is a big decision. Many sites deploy ads with great success, while others not so much. Building relationships and/or making money using real estate on your site can be considered as part of your engagement plan. Your engagement plan should revisited as often as needed to ensure that the best decisions for your site are being made as often as required. Reviewing the pro's and con's of using ads is a great first step.

Direct Ad Agreements

A common practice is to form agreements directly with individual web site owners on the paticulars of exhanging Ad space. Ad spaces are often pre-priced for lease once terms has been set as to length of time, content approval, etc.

Affiliate Programs

Partnering with established brands to form mutually befenifical (financial) relationship is a smart move – ONLY IF – it fits into the goals you have set for your site. Agreements with companies you use or are relevant to your site's content may have an affiliate program.

Ad Exchanges

Ad exchanges allow for ads to be placed into ad inventory where they can be dolled out to the sites of specific target audiences. Google Double-Click is a popular Ad Exchange. More information on their service can be found at:

https://support.google.com/adwords/answer/2472739?hl=en

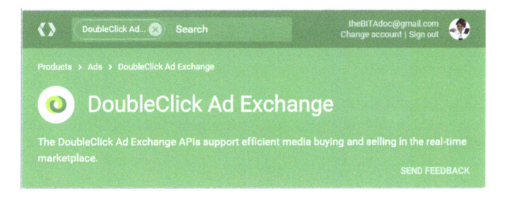

The Pro's of using Ads on your Site

There are many good reasons to run ads on your WordPress site. The use of ads should be reviewed as you develop your engagement plan. Below are a few positives ad impressions can bring to a site.

Building Relationships
Networking in your niche area is important. Finding out who the players in your field will help in building your brand, specifically, where you fit in the current landscape. Building relationships in your industry by exchanging links, ad space, and information on your site can help position your site to be reached by entirely new set of visitors – all of theirs.

Increase Professional Look and Feel of the Site
You have done your due diligence as a new master of your Web site. You have a well-designed sight, with great content, and engaging images. Having well-designed and well-positioned ads on your site can help give the relevance and a professional feel.

Leverage Site Traffic (Income)
Capitalizing on the visitor traffic you have built is a common next step. If your site enjoys established flow of traffic, real estate on the site can be leveraged to open up a stream of income from leasing ad space on your site. This can be a powerful tool in your arsenal when you are ready, Yaro Starak (https://www.entrepreneurs-journey.com/105/making-money-from-your-web site-using-advertising/) tells his readers, "you [should] have about 500-1000 unique visitors per day to your site *at least* before you can start to make real money." From ads on your web site.

The Cons of using Ads on your Site

Ruin Look and Feel of the Site
Ads that are irrelevant to the site's mission, purpose, and content can give visitors the impression that the site lacks focus. Overly intrusive pop-up and poorly designed ads cheapens the experience of the site and may give visitors the impression that your content is of low quality as well. You want ads to enhance, not diminish the quality of the experience while on the site.

Increase Bounce Rate
An unintended consequence of introducing outside content onto your site is the possibility an unrelated ad could drive traffic instead of your content. Once the user realizes they did not land within expected content – they leave.

Reduced Site Speed
Anytime you introduce graphics and animation it affects the performance of your web site.

In the previous chapters you learned how important it is for a WordPress site to be social. In this chapter we will explore ways to expand the footprint of your Web site in ways that encourages user engagement.

In this chapter, you will:

- Learn how to add a blog to your site
- Learn how to add user uploads
- Learn how to add a forum

In this chapter, you will explore ways to use your WordPress site to encourage engagement of the user by expanding footprint of the Web site. In this chapter we will explore the benefit of adding a blog to a traditional site, giving users the ability to add their own content, and adding community forums, in this case, WordPress' go-to forum, BuddyPress.

ADDING A BLOG TO A TRADITIONAL SITE

Adding a blog to a site that only contain static pages of information to drive user interaction on traditional sites is very popular. Eliciting feedback by way of comments gets the user involved and not just experiencing the content externally. Because WordPress is built on a blogging foundation, a blog is easy to incorporate into an existing site that consists only of static pages (traditional). All that is required to create a blog in most templates, is to assign the blog a page in the site and start adding posts and allow comments.

REFRESHER ON WORDPRESS POSTS

Most traditional sites have added to the popularity of their sites by expanding their footprint to add user feedback, articles, offering help, etc. via a blogging platform. Think of WordPress Posts as articles written for your very own newspaper. They are organized in reverse chronological order by the date they were published.

Although blog post information in a beginner topic, now is a good place to do a short refresher. The main folders are January through December and each blog post (article) is listed by the date it was published. Like a newspaper, your posts (articles/stories) reside in sections called categories and can be tagged with words so they can be easily found. For example, Shoes-Women's-Heels-Stack.

They can also be delivered to users as they are published via RSS feeds (we'll discuss those later). Posts are dynamic, which means they are meant to function as a live document. Users are encouraged to interact with posts by leaving comments, liking, and sharing this information. If your posts are for information only comments can always be turned off.

There are many settings that are especially for blogging (posts) in the dashboard. Start by visiting the Settings section.

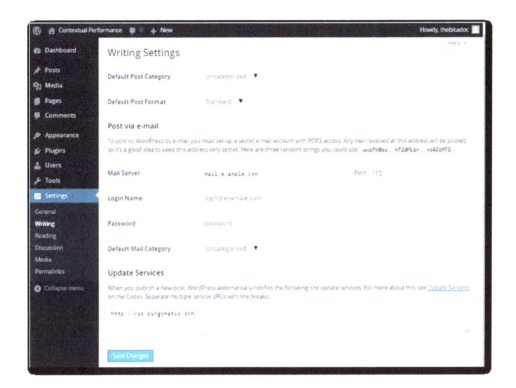

Default Post Category: Remembering that WordPress was initially a blogging tool. All posts that are in the "Default Post Category" will show on the template blog page by default. We will learn how to create new Categories for posts in the Posts section of the text.

If you require the nuts and bolts of creating and displaying post, I recommend the book, Creating a Web Site using WordPress the Beginner's Guide (ISBN - 978-0-692-63203-1) by Dr. Shere L.H. McClamb – *I heard it's really good!*

USER UPLOADS

Allowing users to upload and enjoy their own content on your site can be a great way to not only engage the user, but it also invests them in the creation of the content of the site. This level of interaction comes with more moderation of the content being added to your site. As always, review the pros and cons, complete an analysis as to whether this is a beneficial addition to your site engagement strategy.

There are many different free and for-pay user upload plugins to choose from. Here's one straight out of the WordPress Plugin Directory.

This plugin allows the creation of a Galleries Page where the uploads from individuals are aggregated and displayed.

When the user clicks on the **Gallery Link** they are taken to that gallery when they are then presented with an **Add Photo** link.

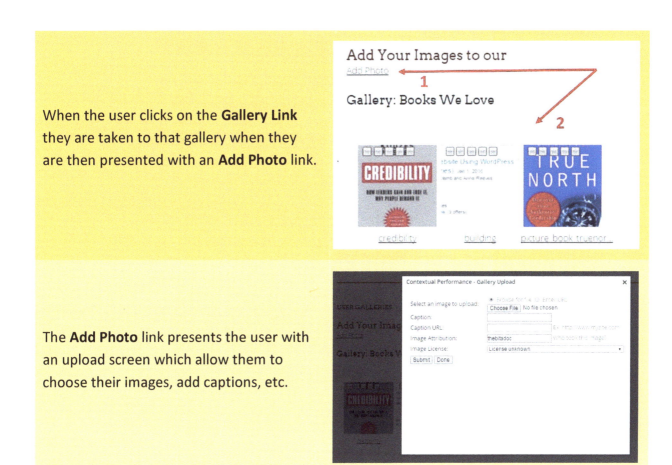

The **Add Photo** link presents the user with an upload screen which allow them to choose their images, add captions, etc.

For a free plugin it includes many of the options you would need to get started. As with all plugins, it is important to read through the instructions and documentation, configure the settings, and tst drive the results prior to releasing it on your site.

BUDDYPRESS – A COMMUNITY FORUM

A social network plugin for WordPress that offers user profiles, activity streams, and groups. Integrate, Login via, and connect with social media options created via a GPL licensed open-source project. Buddy press is similar to WordPress in that it is not only free-to-use, there is a community of developers, users, contributors, etc. constantly working to improve the application.

THE BUDDYPRESS CODEX

The BuddyPress codex is the user manual and support documentation in wiki form for BuddyPress application. In the codex one can learn how to use and troubleshoot BuddyPress features, and plugins. The BuddyPress Codex URL is: https://codex.buddypress.org/.

HELP & SUPPORT

Help and support is also be found in the Codex. The main page is broken into sections from **Getting Started** to Version Releases & **Changelogs**.

 BuddyPress.org

Categories

BuddyCamps

Community

Guest Post

How To

make.wordpress

Meta

News

Screencasts

WordCamps

Sections

The codex is also organized into various sections, which you can check out below:

Components	Versions	Types	Contexts
• Activity	• 2.5.2	• Action	• Developer
• Blogs	• 2.5.1	• Class	• User
• Core	• 2.5	• Extensions	
• Forums (bbPress)	• 2.4.3	• Filter	
• Friends	• 2.4.2	• Function	
• Groups	• 2.4.0	• Language	
• Members	• 2.4	• Legacy	
• Messages	• 2.3.5	• Loop	
• Notifications	• 2.3.4	• Template Tag	
• Settings	• 2.3.3	• Theme Updating	
• XProfile	• 2.3.2		

Resources ranging from beginner to developer available in the Codex. They also offer a hyperlinked, excel-type index.

THE BUDDYPRESS COMMUNITY

There is also access to the community section in the Codex. This includes information on the previous, current, and upcoming releases, changes, information on installation and upgrades. The BuddyPress community is open and anyone is free to contribute to its ongoing success.

Who's Using BuddyPress?

There are sites and blogs that will give you a run-down of who's doing BuddyPress justice out there, here's a couple:

8 New Examples of BuddyPress Powered Communities 2016
https://85ideas.com/blog/best-examples-of-buddypress-web sites/

12 Amazing Examples of BuddyPress Web sites 2015
https://www.sourcewp.com/examples-of-buddypress-web sites/

BuddyPress Themes and Plugins

There are themes and plugins that integrate seamlessly into the WordPress landscape. When using BuddyPress as the community forum on your site you will follow the same instructions when looking for, downloading, and configuring compatible themes and Plugins.

BUDDYPRESS THEMES

To find free BuddyPress themes:

STEP 1.   Go to http://wordpress.org.
STEP 2.   Click on **Themes** on the Navigation bar.
STEP 3.   Type **buddypress** in the search box.

Result: Theme utilizing BuddyPress are displayed.

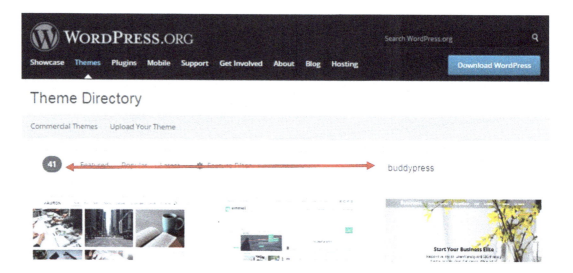

STEP 4.   Hover Over or Click on the site image.

Results:

Sauron *By webdorodo*

Preview   Download

Last updated: **April 11, 2016**

Active Installs: **Less than 10**

Theme Homepage →

Ratings

5 stars		1
4 stars		0
3 stars		0
2 stars		0
1 star		0

Add your review

Support

Got something to say? Need help?

View support forum

Sauron is a responsive WordPress multipurpose theme. This SEO-friendly WordPress theme uses one page scroll and parallax technology with easy set-up sticky menu. It has wide list of customizable features including full-width posts grid, front page builder, full screen lightbox slideshow, layout editor and social sharing options. It is compatible with top WordPress plugins such as WPML(multilingual ready), JetPack, Contact Form 7, bbPress, BuddyPress, Photo Gallery and various e-commerce plugins. A special accent is made on its cross-browser compatibility, mobile friendly design and responsive features. The theme is retina ready with clean flat design. Sauron also can be fully customized to be used for business portfolio, company corporate, commercial, non-profit

Translations

BUDDYPRESS PLUGINS

To search for free BuddyPress plugins, go to the WordPress Codex. Go to the plugins directory and search the word BuddyPress.

Same rules apply for BuddyPress plugins. Make sure the theme is compatible to the version of WordPress you have installed. If not, you will receive an error message here.

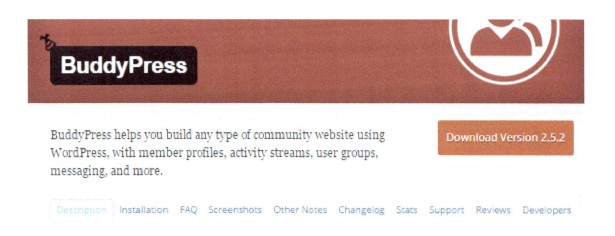

CHAPTER SEVEN: UX & UI

This chapter will teach you to display your posts and pages in ways that are easy for your visitors to find and follow. You will also learn ways to manage your site's users, registration and logins to enhance control as a site's owner

In this chapter, you will:

- Learn the importance of the user experience of a site
- Learn how to create a well-designed interface
- Learn how to control the UX and UI of your web site via themes and frameworks
- Learn how to improve user experience using bandwidth

WordPress is used by thousands to develop traditional web sites. Moving visitors around your site should be carefully planned. Well-designed web sites ensure that as visitors navigate a web site, they always know where they are and have a clear path to get to the information they are looking for. Even though menus can contain pages, posts, and links, pages created in WordPress are only visible on the site via menus and links.

USER EXPERIENCE AND USER INTERFACE DEFINED

Web sites and applications have become complex and interactive depending on systems and processes requiring concrete methods of planning and development to ensure successful outcomes. The development of a web site, even one as straight-forward as WordPress will seem very chaotic and many times it is.

Visitor interaction with your WordPress Web site demands an understanding of the conceptual models of the system, functionality, and label for objects and actions. Although creating a positive experience for the visitor may seem like a clear-cut process, we must take into account that various users have different purposes as they move around the web site.

You are taking on a great responsibility in designing your WordPress site. Cognitive and perceptual psychology is as imperative to allow you to adequately design and evaluate the layout of your site. You may have great ideas for your site and the content you have prepared is too, but how will that translate into your visitor's human perceptual and cognitive abilities. Formal training in behavioral science methodologies is often considered preferred when developing applications but is only considered a basic requirement went designing interfaces for web sites.

As a UX non-professional you should always conduct an analysis of your site's visitor requirements. This can be achieved by documenting and examining how they will access your site by taking into account the various delivery channels and devices. Visitor-centered web site design techniques such as Web analytics, wire-framing, and user stories are used by designers to collect and arrange user information and you should use them too.

Knowing and understanding what the visitor expects from the web site or application will drive the design process to success. Developing good user (visitor) profiles is the first step to any good interface design. You can capture information that pertains to your typical visitor using forms and interviews. The type of information required about the visitor will depend on the type of web site you are creating and how you expect the visitor will interact with. It should be completed very early in the design process and updated accordingly. Visitor-profiles can vary depending on the system they will be used but will usually start begin with the traditionally collected information which includes demographic, socio-economic, education, and technical ability information. The complexity of the visitor-profile is a representation of user knowledge as well as analytical methods and techniques representing how they solve problems.

Determining what layout or design will end in a positive experience requires the you or you UX designer to understand the user's expectations, experiences, emotions, and backgrounds. If a web site or application is not useful or the user is plagued by unmet expectations from the interface your web site, even if it is chocked full of great content, will be considered a failure to those who visit it.

Because the ultimate goal of the UXI designer is to create a web site design that will provide the visitor with a straightforward experience as they interact with technology, UCD (user centered design) process becomes very important. According to the W3C (http://www.w3C.com) the design should focus on usability goals, user characteristics, environment, tasks, and workflow as the user interacts with hardware, software, and web sites.

Interface elements should be placed and grouped in a proximity that the visitor finds intuitive. There is a certain amount of expectation the visitor brings with them as they navigate an interface that is new to them. There are many instances where applications build on familiar layouts and timelines to help the visitor navigate even if the processes and outputs are different.

Visitor Interaction Basics

Before a site visitor can experience all of the content of your site (newsletters, email notifications, etc.) they will need to be registered with the site. In most cases you will not need to adding register and login options to your site. Most WordPress themes are configured with user registration and login links as defaults.

Samples:

Add a registration link to your site:

First you will need to allow users to register to your site:

STEP 1.   Go to the **Settings** link in the Left Main Navigation menu.

STEP 2.   Check **Anyone can register**.

STEP 3.   Choose their role from the **New User Default Role** list.

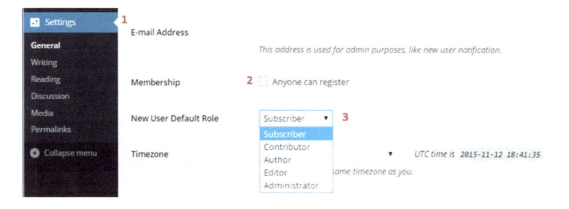

STEP 4.   Click the **Save Changes** button to save your update.

Save Changes

Result: The Register option will appear on your site.

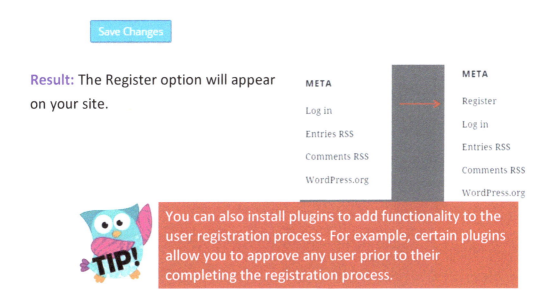

You can also install plugins to add functionality to the user registration process. For example, certain plugins allow you to approve any user prior to their completing the registration process.

Add a registration link to your site:

STEP 1.   Add the following link to your site: http://YourWebiteFullDomainURL/user-registration/

Result: The user will be taken to the default registration screen.

Note: The new user registration screen will look different based on the activated template.

The user will:

STEP 1.   Fill in the **Username** field.

STEP 2.   Fill in the **E-mail** field.

STEP 3.   Click the **Register** button.

Result: The new user will receive the message: Registration complete. Please check your email. This is the same process as adding a new user from the dashboard.

Add a login link to your site:

Add the following link to your site: http://FullWeb siteDomainURL/log-in.php/

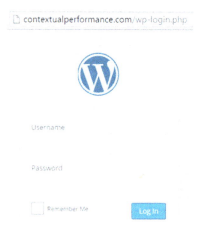

Result: The user will be taken to your site's login screen.

CHARACTERISTICS OF UI

Themes are the foundation of the WordPress site layout. WordPress themes are developed for the average person who wants to build a fully functioning web site using a foundation that they can walk through with step-by-step instructions. The use of themes is one of the elements that makes WordPress so user-friendly. Taking the time to search for and choose the right theme is a major step in planning your site. There are literally thousands of themes to choose from. WordPress is a tool that makes it easier to create a web site, it should not be used a deterrent from doing work it takes to design, create, and maintain a site.

POPULAR PREMIUM THEME MARKETPLACES

themeforest.net/category/wordpress

**templatemonster.com/
wordpress-themes.php**

themify.me/

mojomarketplace.com/themes/wordpress

elegantthemes.com

Choosing the Right Theme for Your Web site

Understanding web site design basics is essential when determining whether a theme is right for your site. Take the time to ask some fundamental web site design questions prior to looking for a theme.

- What is the goal of my web site?
- Who is my audience?
- What messages am I attempting to convey?
- What look and feel do I want for my site?
- Do I require a picture-laden or text-heavy layout?

WordPress Frameworks

Frameworks are a very popular choice for professional front end web designers. All of the following frameworks made it onto ATHEMES.com 12 BEST WORDPRESS THEME FRAMEWORKS 2016 (http://athemes.com/collections/best-wordpress-theme-frameworks/).

POPULAR WORDPRESS FRAMEWORKS

http://www.cherryframework.com/

layerswp.com

diythemes.com

my.studiopress.com/themes/genesis

headwaythemes.com

elegantthemes.com/gallery/divi/

Out of the box functionality and options include:

- Most themes are designed to integrated with WordPress admin;
- You will receive Integrated specialized functions;
- Choice of multiple child themes;
- They will often be optimized for speed and performance;
- They will offer their own specialized set of add-ons and plug-ins;
- Custom CSS and JavaScript panels;
- No white label branding – You can insert your own branding instead of WP or theirs;
- Web site support usually includes extensive documentation and resources.

WHEN THINGS GO WRONG

Very often, especially with new sites and one-click installs you will receive an error when attempting to upload media to your media library (your database). More often than not the reason for the error is that the **Maximum File Upload Size in WordPress** is set to a size less than the files you are attempting to upload. There are a couple of ways to increase the maximum file upload size in your WordPress installation.

First, let's look at the Maximum upload size file you have at this time:

STEP 1.   Go to the **Media Library** and Click the **Add New** media button.

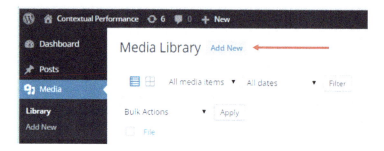

Result: The Maximum upload file size is displayed at the bottom of the **Upload New Media** screen.

STEP 2.   You will need to increase this number. The best way to determine you upload file size requirements is to take an inventory of the files you plan to use in your site. Use the file size of the largest media element.

What size are you going to use?

Now it is time to change your file upload size. To complete this procedure, you will need to access your plain text editor (Notepad++) and FTP Client (FileZilla).

STEP 3.   Open the **Notepad++** application.

First let's check to see if you already have a **PHP.INI** file in your root directory.

STEP 4.   Click on File on the main menu, scroll down and click **Open**.

STEP 5.   Look for PHP.INI. If you find it open it and go to STEP 7.

You do not have a PHP.INI file in your root directory.

STEP 6.   Click on **File** on the main menu, scroll down and click **New**.

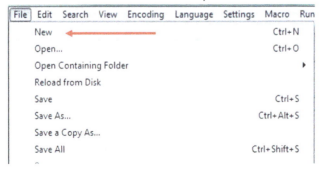

Result: A new coding screen is displayed.

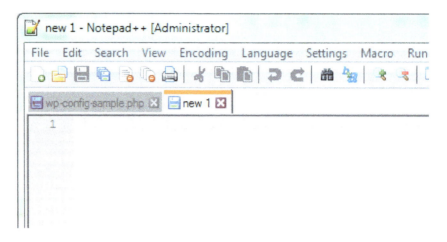

Type:

upload_max_filesize = 10M

post_max_size = 10M

max_execution_time = 300

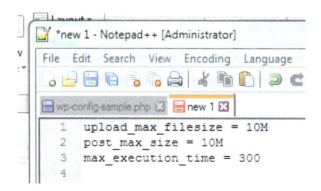

Save this document as **PHP.INI** n your Root Directory

STEP 7.

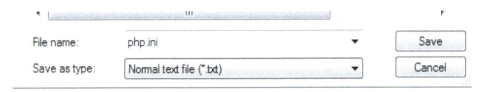

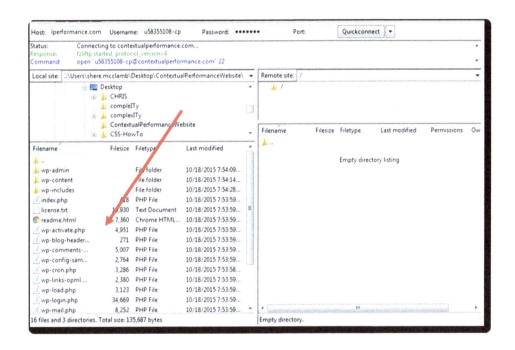

Or you can use the .htaccess METHOD

STEP 1.   Open the **Notepad++** application.

First let's check to see if you already have an .htaccess file in your root directory.

STEP 2.   Click on File on the main menu, scroll down and click **Open**.

STEP 3.   Locate for htaccess. If you find it open it and go to STEP 7.

You do not have an .htaccess file in your root directory.

STEP 4.   Click on **File** on the main menu, scroll down and click **New**.

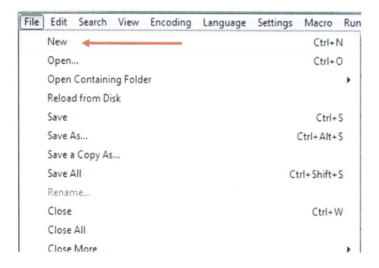

Result: A new coding screen is displayed.

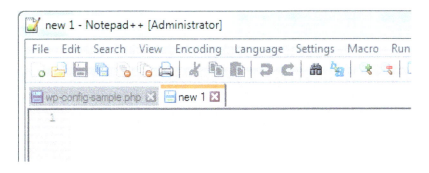

STEP 5.   Type:

php_value upload_max_filesize 10M

php_value post_max_size 10M

php_value max_execution_time 300

php_value max_input_time 300

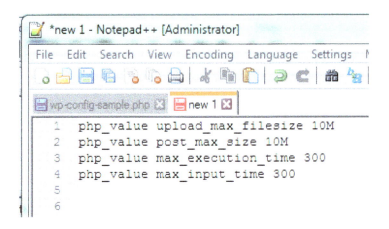

STEP 6.   Save this document .htaccess

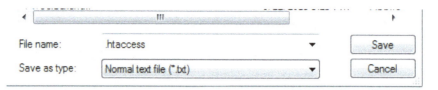

In your **Root Directory**

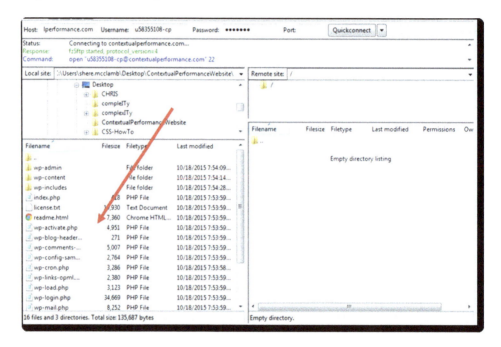

When Plugins Break Your Site

That sounds scary and believe me you will have a pit in your stomach when and if it happens to you. Plugins, as great as they are at expanding the functionality of your site, the fact remains they are created by developers who do not know which other plugins you have installed on your site. Sometimes the coding of plugins bump heads with one another. The problems this causes ranges from problems with a plugin, problems with several plugins, or the worse, you being locked out of your admin panel.

This is of particular issue when you are a front end web site designer. This section walks you through how to deactivate all plugins when you're not able to access the dashboard or WP-Admin.

To complete this procedure, you will need to access your WordPress files:

STEP 1.   Open the **Filezilla** client.

STEP 2.   Connect to you WordPress files. You completed the steps to connect local and remote files in **Creating a Web site using WordPress: The Beginner's Guide** (Chapter 4 – Using the Filezilla Quick Connect Bar).

Using the FileZilla Quick Connect Bar

Step 1. Fill in the information in the quick connect bar.

> **Host**- This is your domain name or URL. **Username**: This is your FTP Username.

> **Password**: This is your FTP User Password. **Port**: The Port for Secure FTP is 22

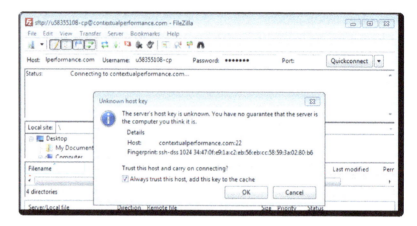

> Make sure to check **Always trust this host, add thus key to the cache**.

> Click the **OK** button.

> Click the **Quickconnect** button to connect to the server.

Result: Once established, the connection can be used to access site files.

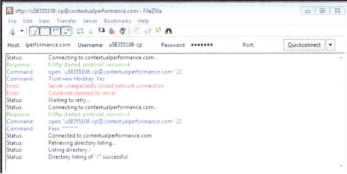

Local files are located on the left side of the interface and the remote files will be uploaded to the right side. Click on the expand icon (+) to view your site files.

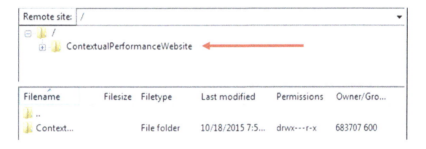

STEP 3.   Navigate to the **/wp-content/** folder in your remote files.

STEP 4.   Rename the plugins folder **deactivateall.plugins**.

Result: Once renamed, all of your plugin will be deactivated on your site. This is going to disable the plugin that causing all of the trouble (and all of the rest too). Now you have the task of activating the plugins one at a time until the culprit is identified.

STEP 5.   Once you have identified the plugin that locked you out – delete it.

CHAPTER EIGHT: MENU MANAGEMENT

You have successfully customized the WordPress site, and now it is time create a navigational menu that is intuitive and drives visitors to the freshest content. The site menu is arguable the most important part of the site.

In this chapter, you will:

- Learn how to build navigation menus
- Learn how to place menus within theme menu locations
- Learn how to place menus in sidebar widgets
- Learn how to work with responsive navigation

The customizations required for creating your site are located in the WordPress dashboard. You will need to log in to the dashboard to customize your new site.

CONTROLLING MENU ITEMS

The Menu screen is accessed from the **Appearance** link in the left navigation menu. Hover over Appearance and then scroll over and select **Menus** from the submenu.

The Menus screen is used to create and configure menus in WordPress regardless of the theme.

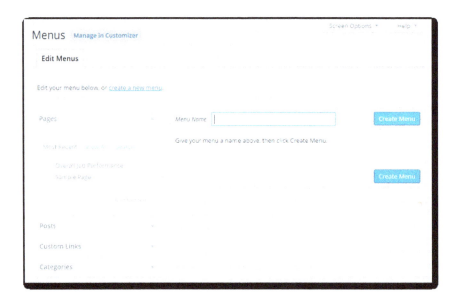

Creating a Hierarchical Menu

Parent Pages (Main Menu Item)

All menu items are automatically placed in the Main Menu in the parent position.

Child Pages (Submenu Item)

A child menu is commonly called a submenu. It is a list of pages that support the page it is nest under.

STEP 1.   Click the menu item that will become the child menu item.

STEP 2.   Drag and drop your way to a menu that reflects the way you want users to move around your site.

Result: The menu item is moved to the subordinate position.

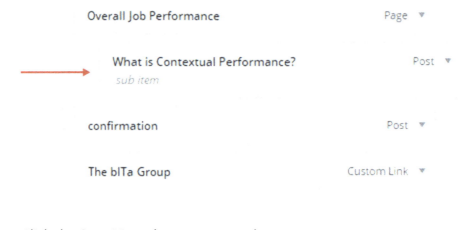

STEP 3.   Click the **Save Menu** button to save the menu.

Result: Main Menu has been updated.

Creating a Title in a Menu with it being a Link

As you saw earlier, you will choose which pages show up on the menus of your web site. What do you do when you have several pages that will be sub-pages that need a title?

STEP 1.   Hover over Appearance in the Left Navigation Bar. Click **Menu** to open the menu.

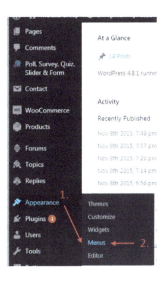

STEP 2.   Locate the **Custom Links** option. Click on the dropdown arrow.

Result: The custom links options open.

STEP 3.   Fill in the **URL** text box with a hashtag (#).

STEP 4.   Fill in the **Link Text** text box with what you want to see on the menu.

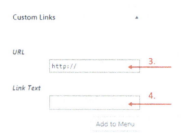

Result: The custom links options open.

STEP 5.   Click the **Add to Menu** button to add the link text to the menu.

Result: The custom links is now in the bottom of the menu. Slide the menu item to where you want it to display in your menu. Follow the instructions to create a sub-menu.

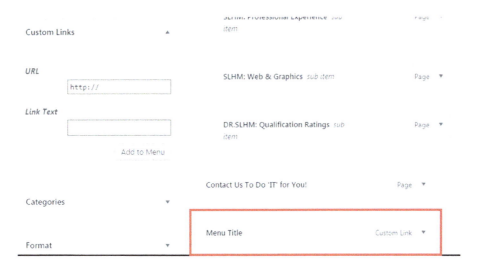

STEP 6.   Click the **Save Menu** button to save the menu.

Result: Main Menu has been updated with a custom title.

MENU LOCATIONS IN A THEME

The locations available for your menu(s) are determined by the theme. This theme offers two menu locations. Because this is the main menu for the site, place a checkmark next to **Primary Menu**.

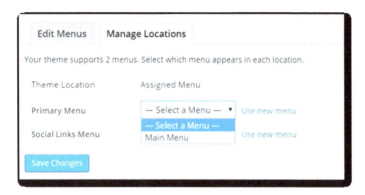

The **Manage Locations** tab gives more options as to menu locations. Here you can view all of the menus you create and place them via dropdown menus.

Adding Items to a Menu

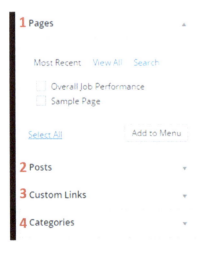

Place the Menu on the Web site

The theme will have predetermined places.

STEP 1.   Click the location where you want your menu to show on the site.

STEP 2.   Click the **Save Menu** button to save the menu.

Result: Main Menu has been saved in the Primary Menu location.

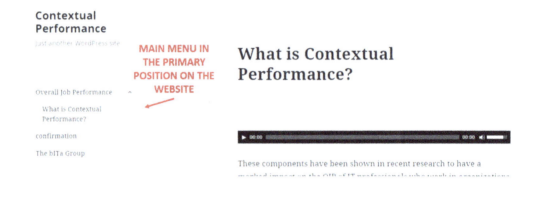

RESPONSIVE NAVIGATION

Responsive navigation is an important part of your WordPress web site plan. It is imperative that you take into account that many of your visitors will not access your site via a desktop computer. The navigation goal for your site is that anyone, regardless of their device will be able to retrieve and have a satisfying experience.

Most up-to-date templates have responsive navigation built in so with this you can by-pass worrying about how to create a mobile-friendly site. You also need to know how your web site will look through these varying modes of viewing.

Let's take a look:

On the Desktop

On a Tablet   On a Cell Phone

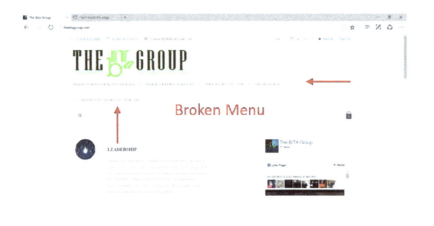

Broken Menu

Menu

As stated earlier, most WordPress templates will have responsiveness built in, but if your template does not then of course, there's a plugin that can handle it.

CHAPTER NINE: SITE OPTIMIZATION & SECURITY

In this chapter you will learn ways to improve you WordPress web site's performance. You can easily build in performance by keeping a few elements in mind when designing your site security and others during maintenance.

In this chapter, you will:

- Learn how to optimize your site content
- Learn how to optimize your site's speed
- Learn how to use the .htaccess file
- Learn how to check for exploits
- Learn the how to hide indexes
- Learn how to use security plugins

At this point WordPress has proven itself to be a winning choice for developing your web site. It is well developed, installed properly, designed exquisitely... what now. As time passes you will undoubtedly add content, images, plugins, etc. to make your site better and better. It is these very upgrades that will degrade the speed of your site. Reversing the slow-down of your site is called optimization.

SITE SPEED

Site speed in an important factor in search engine ranking. As a matter-of-fact Google has place it as an "important" factor in their ranking algorithm. So how will you know your site's speed? How will you know if it is suffering from poor performance? There are a few performance tests you can run to get a better idea of the next steps in this area.

Performance Testing

WordPress.org recommends the following **Tools for Performance Testing:**

Google Developers: PageSpeed Insights	http://developers.google.com/speed/pagespeed/insights/
Mozilla Firefox+ Firebug+ Hammerhead	http://www.mozilla.com/firefox/
	http://getfirebug.com/)
	http://stevesouders.com/hammerhead/
Yahoo! YSlow	http://developer.yahoo.com/yslow/
Google Chrome + Google Speed Tracer	http://www.google.com/chrome
	http://code.google.com/webtoolkit/speedtracer/
Pingdom	http://tools.pingdom.com/
WebPagetest	http://www.webpagetest.org/test
Resource Expert Droid	http://redbot.org/
Web Caching Tests	http://www.procata.com/cachetest/
Port80 Compression Check	http://www.port80software.com/tools/compresscheck.asp
A simple online web page compression / deflate / gzip test tool	http://www.gidnetwork.com/tools/gzip-test.php
Web Page Analyzer	http://www.web siteoptimization.com/services/analyze/

Plugins

The same Plug-ins that are used to increase functionality on you WordPress web site also decrease your site's performance. Cut down on the number of plugins you use with your site. This can be done by prioritizing your functional needs, wants, and nice-to-haves. You can also utilize plugins that pull double duty – killing a couple of birds with one stone. Finally, when removing plugins you don't need or are not using.

Caching

Caching plugins will create static or HTML-like pages out of your posts and pages so that they will render on the screen faster. So instead of WordPress going to the MySQL database to assemble the page or post, it will instead send a snapshot of it. This is great for pages and posts that don't require updating.

Optimizing Images

Images are another drain on optimization. Large images take up a lot of bandwidth and can slow your web site down big-time. When using plugins remember to find the ones that accomplish more than one goal. For example, this plugin optimizes images and help with the alt and title tags!

Shared Hosting

Questions to ask:

- What does my hosting plan include?

- Are they slowing down my bandwidth?

- Am I exceeding my bandwidth?

Themes

Activated Theme

Even though themes are invaluable in the design process, they are packed with images and files that you don't use. You could CAREFULLY get rid of the images and files you don't need for your site. This will definitely help with optimization but I cannot stress enough the importance of moving forward with extreme care.

Old Themes

Also remember to delete the themes you tried and chunked. To do this, open **Themes**.

STEP 1. Hover over **Appearance** and then click on **Themes**.

Result: You should see the currently installed theme as well as the deactivated ones.

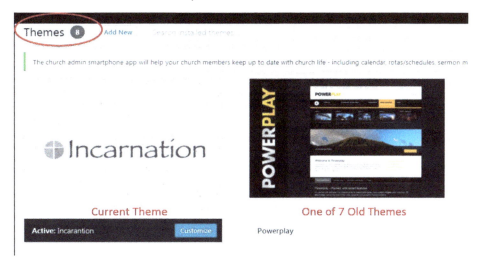

STEP 2.   Click on a deactivated theme.

STEP 3.   Click the **Delete** button in the bottom right corner

STEP 4.   You will receive a message popup asking are you sure you want to delete the them. Click on the **OK** button to confirm.

Result: That's it – Theme Deleted!

PROTECTING YOUR SITE

The on-going security of your site is paramount in keeping your site up and running. Instituting a strong and regular security check is one of the most important tools you can deploy for the health of your site.

Securing directories with .htaccess

First let's check to see if you already have an .htaccess file in your root directory.

STEP 1.   Click on File on the main menu, scroll down and click **Open**.

STEP 2.   Locate for htaccess. If you find it open it and go to STEP 7.

You do not have an .htaccess file in your root directory.

STEP 3.   Click on **File** on the main menu, scroll down and click **New**.

Result: A new coding screen is displayed.

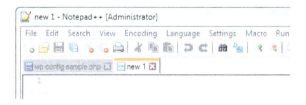

STEP 4.   Type:

```
# secure uploads directory
<Files ~ ".*\..*">
        Order Allow,Deny
        Deny from all
</Files>
<FilesMatch "\.(jpg|jpeg|jpe|gif|png|tif|tiff)$">
        Order Deny,Allow
        Allow from all
</FilesMatch>
```

Result: This denies access to all files but then allows access only to the specified types of images.

STEP 5.   Save this document **.htaccess** in your **Root Directory**

Check for Exploits

 Being vigilant to protect your WordPress web site is an enormous responsibility. According to wpmudev there are over 7.5 MILLION attacks on WordPress sites every HOUR! So how can you protect your site? I recommend scanning your web site for vulnerabilities. We must understand that however vigilant we are in protecting our site, hackers out there have the same amount to cause havoc.

Let's get to what you can do:

- Strengthen usernames and passwords

- Run Security Scans

- Use a Security Monitor with vulnerability Alerts

- Check for Vulnerable Plugins Hide Indexes

::END

www.ingramcontent.com/pod-product-compliance
Lightning Source LLC
Chambersburg PA
CBHW041006050326
40689CB00029B/4988